BOOKS ON STAGECRAFT

Drafting for the Theatre
Dennis Dorn and Mark Shanda

Imaging the Role: Makeup as a Stage in Characterization
Jenny Egan

Stage Rigging Handbook
Jay O. Glerum

Sceno-Graphic Techniques. Third Edition
W. Oren Parker

Theory and Craft of the Scenographic Model
Darwin Reid Payne

Theatrical Scene Painting: A Lesson Guide
William Pinnell

Imaging the Role

Makeup as a Stage in Characterization

Jenny Egan

Southern Illinois University Press

Carbondale and Edwardsville

Edited by Teresa White

Designed by Edward King

Production supervised by Natalia Nadraga

95   94   93   92   1   2   3   4

Library of Congress Cataloging-in-Publication Data

Egan, Jenny.
   Imaging the role : makeup as a stage in characterization
/ by Jenny Egan.
   p. cm.
Includes index.
   1. Makeup, Theatrical. 2. Acting. I. Title
PN2068.E35 1992
792'.027—dc20   90-10375
ISBN 0-8093-1507-6 (pbk.)   CIP

Cover: (*foreground*) character of the Mother in *The Two Executioners* by Fernando Arrabal; (*background*); same actress in street makeup.

*For all young people who are fascinated by the thought
of being both themselves and someone else at the same time.*

*For the professional performer who sits down before the
makeup mirror longing for straightforward, blow-by-blow
directions on what to do with eyes, nose, cheeks, and chin.*

*For teachers, directors, and play producers who know from
experience that makeup is more than a numbers game of
"Color me G–12."*

*And finally for Luther Adler, who taught the writer her
makeup basics, and Stella Adler, who taught her what
makeup is in aid of—in appreciation of what they gave.*

Contents

Preface

Imaging the Role is both a student's introduction and a working actor's guide to the theory and practice of making up for the part. It includes a concise, easily understood exploration of the connection between makeup and character. While its content may be obvious to some, many experienced performers are not fully aware of what makeup can accomplish. For them, *Imaging* will replace passive dependence on the makeup artist with a personal expertise that completes their mastery of their craft. And experience, after all, is relative. Everyone is "experienced" at making out an income tax form, but who would not welcome with shouts of joy some clear, easy-to-follow directions that would demystify the process!

Most makeup manuals give extremely sketchy treatments of theatrical characterization, focusing almost exclusively on the techniques of applying paint. *Imaging* supplies detailed instructions on cosmetic application but only after thoroughly establishing the relationship of appearance to character. It shows the reader how to reach decisions on what the character looks like, and it outlines the means by which the image in the performer's mind is translated to his or her face. An aim of the book is to demonstrate makeup's ability to convey character subtleties without masking or inhibiting the moment-to-moment play of facial expression.

Imaging deals as much with the craft of acting as with makeup. It places the genesis of the character's image not in the wake of the rehearsal period, as a sort of hasty afterthought, but at the first or second reading of the play. Once the character image begins to materialize, it remains the actor's constant companion. Its shifts and changes parallel the growth of the inner character, keeping pace with the performer's deepening understanding of the role.

This indissoluble bond between inner and outer character is recognized instinctively by all good actors but is seldom verbalized and is frequently not dealt with in makeup classes as thoroughly as it deserves. A premise of this book is that the thoughts, actions, and events that shape personality leave traces on the face, teasing and pulling the features into a mould as individual as a fingerprint. *Imaging the Role* rejects the simplistic notion of character "types" and stresses the uniqueness of each human (or nonhuman) being the actor is called upon to play. It sets forth techniques for precisely defining this uniqueness and for capturing its essence in grease and pancake. And because this book sees the makeup process as more than something that happens to the actor from the neck up, it will emphasize the total visual impact of the character on the audience, discussing in depth the contribution of props and costume to the overall effect.

To the writer's knowledge, *Imaging* is the first book that gives explicit directions on how to synthesize a character's visual image from the impressions generated by the actor's imagination and the script. It is not a historical study, not a definitive technical encyclopedia for the professional makeup artist, not an anthology of clothing, jewelry, and hairstyles. It is a portable manual that, as it's subtitle says, views makeup as a stage in characterization. It was written mainly to help performers, students, and teachers bridge the gap between understanding a role and expressing that understanding in tangible form. Its writing has been a quest for universals, an effort to identify what principles are lasting and will therefore be true for the theatre of tomorrow as well as today. Many of its examples are drawn from the classics. For those who think of classics as the "then," not the "now," this may pose a problem, yet theatre journals reveal that over 70 percent of produced plays are revivals of standard classics from the Greeks to Miller, Williams, Hansberry, and Hare. Furthermore, a large proportion of these productions are done "straight," that is, in period with some attempt to keep the play in its historical context.

Imaging is designed to make its readers think. It urges them to make connections and draw conclusions about what they want to do with their faces. It does not dwell exhaustively on warts or the latest in ethnic fashions, although these things may be important for a particular role. Rather, it tries to elucidate the principles that enable a black or white actor to look like a Chinese, a Mexican Indian, an Australian aborigine, or Ariel or Caliban. It is not for those mainly interested in special effects and Halloween heads but for the serious performer who is, by definition, concerned with essences rather than superficialities. Warts are fine but first there must be a face to put them on. The detail is always part of a whole.

The advice of the author, a veteran of all types of plays from musical comedy to documentary drama, is supplemented by extensive commentary from other working actors, many of them leaders in the field. Exercises and problems for the student are also included for those who are using the book as a teaching text. Singers, lecturers, and dinner speakers will find many helpful hints throughout, for while *Imaging*'s main thrust is stage characterization, there is much in the book to interest any individual who goes before an audience to instruct or entertain. Finally, professional makeup artists will find food for thought in *Imaging*. Although it is not intended to train them to pass the union exam (there are other books to do that), it will provide deeper insight into how an actor thinks and the process by which the image develops from the inside out.

The writer wishes to thank the following individuals and organizations for their help: Brad Woolbright, Dan Duro, Claudia Chavez, Jill Lindgren, and Theodore A. Stark of the Santa Fe Opera; Tom Wei; Jose C. Ortega and family; Marsha C. Bol; Barbara Mauldin, acting curator of Latin American Folk Art, Museum of International Folk Art, the International Folk Art Foundation Collections at the Museum of International Folk Art, Santa Fe; Richard Fitch; the Tom Riggs Gallery; John and Gina Kraul; Andrew Shea, artistic director of the New Mexico Repertory Theatre; John Weckesser and Cheryl Odom of the College of Santa Fe Department of Drama. Special appreciation is due to Kenney Withers, director, along with Teresa White and Natalia Nadraga, of the Southern Illinois University Press; Robert S. Phillips; Reed Campbell; Pat Martin of Visions Photo Lab; Maria Benitez; my students at the Stella Adler Conservatory of Acting, NYU, SMU, and Columbia University; Ron Grinage; Curtis Brown and for his unfailing encouragement and sheer endurance, William McGonigle.

Introduction

Actors in search of their characters run a tight marathon. With four to six weeks to countdown, they are racing the clock. Irrascible, frequently irrational, they plunge blindly through a dark forest from which they have only the director's word that they will ever emerge.

It is a devious journey, this quest for another human being who exists someplace "out there" but refuses to be found, often until the night before opening, sometimes not even then. Stella Adler tells of her father's twenty-year search for Othello. James Earl Jones speaks of discovering new facets of that role even after playing it in six productions. The most one dares to hope for is a dead heat: to cross the finish line with the character firmly in hand by the first public preview.

It is unthinkable that after so much expense of time and energy, the character should prove headless, yet that is what many actors give birth to: an apparition that speaks, walks, and dresses in a distinctive manner but has no face of its own. A strange oversight.

Frustrating and unpredictable, the characterization process is also one of the most demanding imaginable, for it frequently requires nothing less than the total reconfiguring of the player's normal appearance and personality. No serious performer can afford to ignore the creative and practical role that makeup plays in this process. Picture this:

1. You are set on directing a script about the American occupation of Japan (six characters: four men, two women) for the town community theatre. Three of the characters are Japanese. There are no Japanese in your town.

2. You have just received a script in the mail from your agent with a note, "Take a look at Molly McGuire." Eagerly, you flip to the Cast of

Characters, run a finger down the page, and discover that Molly McGuire is—a horse.

3. Lips smugly pursed in the character of a middle-aged matron, you catch the sound of the curtain hitting bottom and sprint to your dressingroom. On matinee days the two one-acts on the bill are played back to back without an intermission. You have three minutes to change costume and return in the part of a twelve-year-old child.

4. A production is announced in which live actors will interact with a simultaneous telecast of their own gigantic images projected across the upstage wall. The live makeups must also be suitable for video.

These actual situations exemplify the need for a mastery of makeup theory and technique appropriate to the fast-moving, mixed-media theatre of today. In that theatre, every character deserves a face. Salome danced for, and received, the head of John the Baptist. Why is it that so many of us are willing to accept less for equal work?

There has been, in fact, a recent rebellion against stage makeup. Many post-Stanislavsky actors abandoned it because it was thought, if unfairly, to restrict the play of emotion and give the face a masklike, dead look at odds with the "natural" vitality of the performer. Of course, the last thing any actor wants is a thick, puddinglike overlay that hardens into a shell an armadillo would be proud of. This is what makeup was in the eighteenth century, when Lady Sneerwell objected to the careless manner in which the Widow Ochre caulked her wrinkles, and Lady Teasle compared her friend "Lady Stucco" to a kind of French fortune cookie that "one cracks for mottos." Today's grease sticks and creams are lighter and more transparent than the earlier ones, and pancake can be applied in the thinnest washes. Latex and plastics have brought prostheses into common use, supplementing or replacing the intractable pink putty that was once the bane of every character actor's existence.

Another factor contributing to the slackening of interest in stage makeup was the replacement of the doll-featured Hollywood ideal by more realistic images of Everyman. With the desegregation and civil rights movements came broader acceptance of ethnic diversity. It became less necessary for everyone to conform to a single standard of beauty. Big ears, outsized noses, receding hairlines—none of these were any longer bars to movie stardom or the financial rewards of television. Stage speech and movement became whatever was the performer's personal norm. This development dovetailed neatly with another outgrowth of the modern theatre, typecasting. Patently, if the face was "right" to begin with, there was no need to, as the French say, "faire des têtes"—do heads.

Historically, balance has always tended to reestablish itself somewhere between extremes, and this appears to be happening in the contemporary theatre. Directors increasingly are calling for versatility, command of language, a sense of style. New plays demand a breathtaking range of characterization stretching from humanoids of all types and times to phantasmagoria, cartoon creations, domestic animals, and public transportation. Now that production costs are routinely figured in the millions, producers are less tolerant of ineptness, particularly as it affects the "look" of a show. Today, as never before, it behooves the performer to know what makeup can do and how to make it work for the character and the play.

Instructions on makeup application are widely available, but the conceptualizing process is less known and nowhere clearly documented in actors' language. There is need for information in this area that can free the performer from inevitable dependence on a makeup artist who joins the show for dress rehearsals. Knowledgeable and skilled though these craftspeople are, they do not invest weeks or months eating, waking and sleeping with the part. You do. Would you wish another to decide in a moment how to act your role?

For better or worse, makeup is wedded to the acting process. It cannot easily be detached from it and delegated to a nonperformer with satisfactory results. It is too personal a business. Many actors have found that allowing someone else to slather them with #F-4-C is a little like letting them use one's toothbrush. Far preferable, whenever possible, for the performer, in concert with the director, to assume responsibility for the growth of the character image from its origin in the first impressions of the play, through its final realization in paint, pancake, and hair. Part I, "Concept," analyzes that process step by step, showing how it parallels the building of the inner character. It offers the advice of professionals on specific makeup problems and ingenious solutions that have been found for them. Samples taken from play texts are explored for clues to the visual image, and sources are given for observation and research on character, nationality, period, and style. There are sections in both parts I and II on costume elements and personal props that are extensions of the makeup and on moving between ethnic groups. Stylized and period makeups are treated as organic expressions of the play's theme and content. Part II, "Execution," is structured as a convenient actor's "Manual" for handy reference, so that the book can be tossed into a makeup kit and used as a guide to application on the job. "The Manual" gives clear directions on the techniques of sculpting with paint and plastic to look better, worse, older, younger, healthy, sick, of this world, or extraterrestrial.

Part I

Concept: An Actor's Approach to Makeup

1

The Whys and Wherefores
of Makeup

Reasons for Wearing Makeup

To the question, Why wear makeup onstage? glib replies spring easily to mind: because the script calls for a brunette and you're a blond; because they couldn't find an Oriental for the Chinese butler; because the horse mask didn't get done in time. From the examples given in the Introduction, it is plain that makeup can save the day in many situations on which a performer's job depends. There are more compelling reasons, however, that derive from the nature of the acting process itself.

1. *To alter physical features to conform to character.* Physical transformations invariably accompany those inner adjustments the actor makes to conform his personality to that of the character. Makeup renders these physical changes visible.

2. *To provide the audience with visual signposts.* How the character looks is, of course, crucial to the impression the character makes on the viewers. In our society, for example, delicate features convey the notion of innocence, fragility, and refinement. This is not fortuitous but the result of centuries of human interaction. When, in an early film, Yul Brynner seized Deborah Kerr's abundant tresses and rasped, "It takes generations to grow hair like that!" he was commenting on on an entire social class and the products of its leisured life-style. The images of Mr. T, Michael Jackson, Hunter, and James Rockford on our television screens confirm that physical characteristics act as signposts within a particular culture,

3

and the information they convey is picked up instantly by the members of that culture, on sight. Although some visual cues have developed into clichés and stereotypes, many others can be found that provide a legitimate means of evoking in the audience's mind the desired character image. As in most things, taste and sensitivity will guide the performer to make wise choices.

3. *To give the actor psychological protection*. Makeup, in that it is a disguise, armors the actor against embarrassment and inhibition. It lends the performer a temporary shield behind which he feels free to lay bare his soul. Even nonperformers find release in assuming "false" faces on Halloween. As the proprietress of a costume and mask shop notes, "It's a fantasy to dress up in costume and makeup. People want to experience being someone else." The French matinee idol Yves Montand recalled his reluctance to assume the part of an old man: "Let the years do their job," he told his wife, Simone Signoret, "Why do I have to anticipate?" But when he put on a mustache, he felt "fine." "I feel suddenly like my ancestors. . . . Hiding behind a mustache helped a lot." A critic for the *New York Times* commented on the same phenomenon in relation to Hume Cronyn. "Give Mr. Cronyn a wig, mustache and glasses and he is about the best character actor in the business."

Audiences take special delight in discovering familiar actors they have failed to recognize under a skillful makeup. Their pleasure is equaled by the performer's glee at eluding self-disclosure. The actress who replaced Anne Bancroft in the Boston production of *The Devils,* in ordinary life a plain woman with unremarkable features, relishes to this day being mistaken, while awaiting her first entrance backstage, for a beautiful dancer who was also a member of the cast. Comedian Robert Morse tells the story of a woman who had known him in high school demanding her money back after seeing him in *Tru,* declaring loudly, "I've known Bobby all my life—that wasn't him!"

Comments by Successful Performers

Actors, directors, and writers have demonstrated keen awareness of the importance of the visual image. Liviu Ciulei saw the trolls in *Peer*

Gynt not merely as monsters but as heightened images of Victorian respectability, boarish parodies of mannered middle-class self-righteousness. Ellen McLaughlin's Hedda at the Berkeley Repertory Theatre developed the metaphor of "a very nervous, overbred racehorse." As a playwright, McLaughlin starts not with the narrative but with an image that is "evocative in some way I don't understand." José Ferrer states: "I don't think actors in this country know nearly enough about makeup as we should." Tony Randall concurs, commenting in a letter to the writer, "You and I know, but do 'the rest' know that putting on a real character makeup requires some little skill and can be taught and acquired without too much difficulty; BUT finding or developing or creating a character and then expressing it in makeup, ah, that's something else again." Andrew Shea, who has won generous National Endowment support for his adventuresome direction of the classics and his premieres of Tony Award-winner Mark Medoff's plays, sees costume and makeup as very much a part of the total picture. "To me," he says, "they go together. The way a character looks, dresses himself, combs his hair, has a scar, has been beaten up—these are all makeup matters, but to me they are part of one issue—the character." Shea might occasionally bring in a makeup specialist for difficult plays like *The Elephant Man*, but he feels that "a lot of this is the actor's job. Professional actors who've been around for awhile get pretty proficient on their own and to the director that's an advantage. Often the actor is the best judge of what he should look like and will give me some very good ideas about the outside of the character." College Performing Arts Department chairman John Weckesser requires freshmen to take makeup courses before going on to any other aspects of performing. He stresses the importance of deriving the makeup from inner character: "Makeup isn't going to do a thing if it's on an empty shell."

Not all actors are comfortable with using makeup to help create the character. Dame Sybil Thorndike thought it superfluous. "I am a very unmakeup-y person," she told the the writer shortly before her death. "I think you've got everybody inside you. You're hampered by your outside, but you can do away with that by thinking. A little around the eyes and mouth . . . your thought does the rest."

Ironically, those who disclaim the need for makeup most

vociferously are often renowned for their deft and imaginative use of it. Alec Guinness is a prime example. Agreeing to be questioned at his home outside London about his views on makeup, the notoriously shy Guinness suddenly changed his mind, leaving his interviewer stranded miles from transportation, in the middle of the English countryside. Later, he explained: "I doubt if I could say anything of the remotest interest to you about makeup. I just do it instinctively, without going into any great psychological searchings. . . . What is more, for many years now I have tried to keep it to a minimum." In fact, no actor ever displayed greater selectivity in the choice of makeup details than Mr. Guinness, of whom more in a later chapter.

What's in a Face?

This a question on which it is hard to find agreement. Shakespeare is full of cautions about judging people by their faces. Like Nero Wolfe's assistant, Archie Goodwin, his characters are continually trying to guess who, in a gathering of people is the murderer, but are usually unable to see behind the public mask that hides the real person from view. Modern experiments with showing people pictures and asking them to separate the criminals from the law-abiding citizens seem to indicate that a Supreme Court justice is all too easily confused with a safecracker.

Many would agree with Duncan that "there is no art to find the mind's construction in the face." And yet—advertising in America is founded on the assumption that people respond in particular ways to a certain cast of features, to looks which they consider friendly or threatening, familiar or strange, happy or discontented. Poets tell us the eyes are the windows of the soul (e.g., the eyes in figure 1). Novelists write stories about people whose faces, like that of Dorian Gray, mirror lives of evil, suffering, or toil.

Newspaper reports of famines, life under dictatorship, and the like, afford daily pictorial evidence that the thoughts, actions, and events that shape a personality leave their mark on the features, imposing a unique configuration without precedent or sequel. No two faces, not even those of identical twins, are precisely the same. Each is an up-to-date product

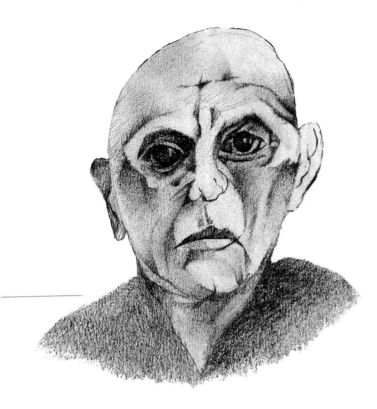

Fig. 1. After a self-portrait by Ivan Albright made in the hospital shortly before his death (Reed Campbell).

of heredity, time, and the twists of Fortune. Richard II, regarding his deposed face in a glass, asks:

> No deeper wrinkles yet? hath sorrow struck
> So many blows upon this face of mine,
> And made no deeper wounds? (4.1)

Nevertheless, his wife notices the change in him at once:

> But soft, but see, or rather do not see,
> My fair rose wither. (5.1)

War is a notorious molder of faces:

> The months of wincing at snipers' bullets, the sleepless nights, and the constant strain of looking for trip wires had aged him. Behind his glasses, Crowe's eyes were as dull as an old man's.[1]

1. Philip Caputo, *A Rumor of War* (New York: Ballantine: 1986), 292.

One soldier said long afterward that the very appearance of the army had changed, as if everything that had happened looked out of the faces of the marching men.[2]

Facial response to situations of the moment can be inhibited with practice but not the ingrained marks of life's inexorable passage over the years. And of course, the actor, unlike the portraitist, does not seek to freeze a fleeting expression in paint. A successful makeup ensnares not the mutable smile or frown that comes and goes like the weather but the private persona who grimaces at life or welcomes it from deep within. The telltale signs of character may be extremely subtle and hard to detect, but they are there and perceiving them, we judge that someone is chronically frightened, harried, nervous, serene, inquisitive, or commanding. Makeup is the means by which these miniscule indications can be spotlighted and enlarged to become visual signals that audiences can recognize even through strong light and over considerable distance.

Makeup's Five Functions

Confusion about the efficacy of stage makeup is perhaps best dispelled by a clear understanding of each of makeup's quite distinct functions. A list of them reveals that the aim of makeup varies with the situation.

1. To counteract the bleaching effects of light and distance on facial color (especially pertinent to large theatres)

2. To restore the third dimension to features that light and distance tend to flatten, while leaving those features esentially unchanged

3. To "beautify" the face without altering the personality it reflects (i.e., corrective makeup)

4. To give oneself a new persona with new features, that is, to characterize

5. To create a nonhuman, fantasy, or masklike outer image suitable to a wholly imaginary being

Obviously, the first two functions are merely practical solutions to well-known technical phenomena. They are discussed more fully in "The

2. Bruce Catton, *A Stillness at Appomattox* (New York: WSP, 1958), 156.

Manual" (part II). The third goal is of doubtful validity in the theatre but is often sought after and applies well to the lecture platform and to interviews. It is dealt with in detail in chapter 14.

Four and five are central to the actor's craft. Fulfilling them demands not only a high degree of technical competence but also profound knowledge of the character and grasp of the play's style. They are the chief reason why makeup is an actor's indispensable tool. Let us examine them more closely, looking first at characters of this world and then at those that go a step beyond.

Study Projects

1. Examine the daily newspaper for three days running and clip out faces of people who have undergone trauma. Write down what you observe in their features or posture that seems to you an outgrowth of the stress (or relief from stress) they have undergone.

2. On your next subway or bus ride or visit to a shopping mall, spend fifteen minutes studying the faces of people. Try to guess what kind of lives they lead. Take notes and justify every guess by recording the details you observe that lead you to each conclusion.

2

That Certain Face: Commencing the Search for the Visual Image

The Fallacy of "Old Age #1"

Commercial makeup companies foster the belief that creating a makeup, like winning the lottery, is merely a question of picking the right numbers. Cosmetics for the stage are therefore given suitably enticing names and a number that is meant to facilitate ordering by catalog. Thus, if you are hired to play a man of eighty-two, you are exhorted to send for something called "Old Age #1." If your character is sickly, you order "Sallow Old Age"; if he makes his living chopping wood, you can choose "Ruddy Old Age" or "Egyptian."

The trouble with this system of codification is twofold: *a)* it is totally subjective, and *b)* whoever labeled the paints was obviously colorblind. In actual practice, you can seldom tell from the catalog description what shade will greet your eyes when you remove the lid of a tin or push the grease from its plastic or metal tube. Pancake has provided another method of application, but the same purple prose continues to describe the available colors: "Aztec Orange," "Pretty Lady," "Mellow Mandarin," "Dracula Gray." The fault, of course, is not in the identifying name but in the simplistic notion that a particular shade of paint holds the key to instant character. Generations of young actors have been led to conclude that people of a given age or ethnic origin are clones of one another and can therefore be arbitrarily colored red, yellow, or pink without the necessity for further thought. Much to the contrary, the wide range of styles and new forms in the contemporary theatre impose a special responsibility on the performer to make personal choices based on knowledge, investigation and experiment. The search for the character's image is a highly personal odyssey. It cannot be undertaken by proxy. However, the actor will find abundant help along the way by knowing where to look.

Sources for the Visual Image

Mining for Gold in the Text

The author's right to be heard. In the fierce competition to come up with novel interpretations of old and new plays, modern actors and directors have led the poor author a merry chase. Not unlike rebellious adolescents, many intentionally spurn the writer's helping hand and proceed to hack a course that brings them into direct conflict with the text. At this point, their guiding principle seems to be, "Cut what doesn't fit and make the rest conform." The result is a new play, whether the novelty is acknowledged or ignored. Such was a college production of *The Bacchae* in which King Pentheus' first line was changed to "F——you, Citizens of Thebes." So also the production of *Romeo and Juliet* in Holland in which only thirty lines of Shakespeare were left intact. In the discussion that follows, the author is assumed to have an inalienable right at least to a fair hearing. Let us look at some of the things the playwright is likely to say that might suggest an image for the character.

Stage direction database. Sean O'Casey describes Mrs. Gogan in act 1 of *The Plough and the Stars* in these terms:

> She is a doleful-looking little woman of forty, insinuating manner and sallow complexion. She is figety and nervous, terribly talkative, and has a habit of taking up things that may be near her and fiddling with them while she is speaking. Her heart is aflame with curiosity, and a fly could not come into nor go out of the house without her knowing.

In this single paragraph are clues to the character's age, health, size, skin color, personal mannerisms, habitual facial expression, disposition, typical attitude, and most consuming interest.

George Bernard Shaw is even more explicit: his stage directions rival his prologues in length and specificity:

As far as the candlelight and his unwashed, unkempt condition make it possible to judge, he is a man of middling stature and undistinguished appearance, with a strong neck and shoulders, a roundish, obstinate looking head covered with short, crisp bronze curls, clear quick blue eyes and good brows and mouth, a hopelessly prosaic nose like that of a strong-minded baby, trim soldierlike carriage and energetic manner, and with all his wits about him in spite of his desperate predicament—even with a sense of humor of it, without, however, the least intention of trifling with it or throwing away a chance. (*Arms and the Man*, act 1)

Whether the actor needs or wants such rigid guidelines is debatable. They leave little room for creating a character along similar lines but with features other than those the author has envisioned. On the theory that an interpretive artist must have room to interpret, many actors begin the study of a play by crossing out all stage directions. Things like "weeping copiously," for example, are instantly expunged, for by the time the player is ready to perform the role, he or she is usually able to guess better than the author where the tears will fall. Still, for those who feel more comfortable staying in close visual "sync" with the playwright, stage directions provide an easily accessible database on which to draw for makeup decisions.

Another character's description of your character. Not all dramatists, however, are given to painting meticulous verbal portraits of their characters. Shakespeare's stage directions, when they exist at all, are terse and noncommittal; information that images the character comes through in other ways. One of his favorite techniques is to let one character describe another. Allowance, of course, should always be made for who is speaking. "Thou elvish-marked, abortive rooting hog," say Margaret of Richard III (1.3). His own mother calls him a toad (4.4) and limns his character from childhood on in these words:

Techy and wayward was thy infancy;
Thy school days, frightful, desperate, wild and furious;
Thy prime of manhood daring, bold and venturous;
Thy age confirm'd, proud, subtle, sly and bloody,
More mild, but yet more harmful, kind in hatred;
What comfortable hour canst thou name
That ever grac'd me in thy company?

A toad, then, but with these special attributes. A rooting hog that savages with refined cunning acquired with practice.

Ophelia's description of Hamlet offers a similar mixture of imagery and psychological insight (3.1): "The courtier's, soldiers, scholar's eye, tongue, sword. . . . The glass of fashion and the mold of form/The observed of all observers. . . . That unmatch'd form and feature of blown youth." Mother Courage needs only one brief sentence to describe her daughter, the mute Katrin: "She's not so pretty anyone would want to ruin her."

Your character's speeches. Another way that information about the prevailing face-set of a character may be deduced is through the character's own remarks. Like Mother Courage, Oedipus is succinct but accurate: "I have an ungovernable temper." In the same vein, Othello at the end of his life sees clearly into his own soul:

> then must you speak
> Of one that lov'd not wisely, but too well
> Of one not easily jealous, but, being wrought,
> Perplex'd in the extreme.

Physical givens. Finally, there are physical "givens" that are not subject to interpretation and must be present recognizably in the final make-up. Such things as Bardolph's red nose in *Henry V,* Katrin's scar and Mélisande's hair may be stylized, but they cannot be omitted, although there is often leeway as to size, shape, color, and placement of the feature.

Influence of Period and Style

When Joseph Papp first made mix-and-match periods fashionable, purists were outraged. Since then, generations of theatregoers have cut their teeth on turn-of-the-century *As You Like Its, Hamlets* set in Cuba, and Roman soldiers wearing Fascist black shirts, trench coats, and dungarees. This fiesta of styles has made it difficult for holdouts to maintain that there is such a thing as style and to speak of period integrity. Still, there is something vaguely disturbing about a Victorian schoolgirl in lipstick or a pioneer woman with plucked eyebrows. Perhaps it comes down to this: if, by putting a play in a certain period, we wish to say something significant about that period, or its relevance to the play, then it becomes important to reflect the era with some accuracy. Obviously, the life-style of a pioneer woman did not admit of plucked eyebrows, therefore their absence reveals much about the character and environment of nineteenth-century women on the American frontier.

Fashions in every period of history have a distinctive look, and models for them may be found handily in paintings of the time. From the nineteenth century on, photographs and advertisements provide additional examples of fashions in makeup and dress (see chapter 18 and appendixes B–G).

Director's and Designer's Input

Good directors can, with a single phrase, often cause the character to materialize before the actor like a rabbit out of the magician's hat. Stella Adler's description of the face of Elizabeth I is such a phrase: "a mind surrounded by a graveyard." So is Andre Serban's vision of the guardian priestess Norma as the Statue of Liberty.

Similarly, the costume designer's inspired rendering of a character's clothing often jars the pieces into place for an actor groping for a coherent image. This is especially true of designers who indicate the the character's habitual posture and who include in their renderings personal props such as canes, crutches, spectacles, and riding crops (fig. 2). Set designers, by capturing the essence of the character's environment, can also aid the actor to visualize the person who lives in those surroundings. Seeing the stark blue-whiteness of a Wolfgang Roth design for a hospital room in a play about a terminally ill woman suggested immediately to the present writer the look of the character's face as she approached her final hours. The best kind of theatre results from a close collaboration. As Vanessa Redgrave put it, one builds a character by "getting the input of a lot of people."

Outside Sources: The Actor's Research

Direct observation. Everything the actor sees or experiences throughout the rehearsal period abets the imaging process. Everywhere performers go, they look for what they can make use of in the world around them. What they cull is added to what is already present in conscious and

Fig. 2. The actor Potier in *Le Ci-devant Jeune-homme,*
nineteenth-century print (collection of the author).

subconscious mind through a kind of winnowing action in which the kernel is seized and the chaff blown to the wind, or carefully filed for use in another role.

Not everything is left to serendipity, however. Conscientious performers learn to look in likely places for artistic nourishment. If one is playing the part of a terminally ill person, the director can often arrange a visit to a hospital ward. If the character is a member of a particular ethnic group, the actor will find himself in neighborhoods where people of that group live or work. When in search of an object of a particular period, a tour of museums in the area can be rewarding, especially if you take a camera or small sketchbook on your reconaissance.

Books and pictorial sources. Often, it is impractical to travel to where the person or object under study can be viewed. In this case, books and pictures of people, places, architecture, and objects of all kinds become the major resource. Picture collections in public libraries will usually allow takeouts or will permit you to photocopy what you need for a small fee.

Starting a picture file. Inevitably, you will want to start your own picture file, or morgue, into which you can drop anything that catches your interest from magazines, newspapers, and handouts you pick up or receive in the mail. As you come across these treasures, house them in file folders, well indexed according to the classifications you find most helpful. This writer's system runs the gamut from "African Cultures" and "Aborigines" to "Children" and "Churches" on down to "Watteau" and "Wigwams." Into it are funneled circulars showing starving Ethiopian mothers, advertisements for Chippendale furniture, a friend's postcard from Arizona, and several months of a calendar featuring Victorian glass. A theatrical swipe file grows geometrically on the assumption that "you never know when you can use something like that," so save everything.

Factors in Arriving at the Visual Image

When and how you can use what you have gathered is explained in chapter 3. In preparation for that discussion, you will want to be thinking about the following list.

Eleven Factors to Consider

1. Environment
   Living space (cave? mountaintop?)
   Work environment (sewing = squint, farming = sunburn)
   Pastime environment (skier? bookworm?)
2. Ethnic group or national origin
3. Health (If sick, what disease? drink? drugs?)
4. Psychological factors
   Basic state of mind (happy? worried? restless?)
   Temporary upsets and lengh of time endured (habitual frown, tremor, tic?)
   Emotional pressures (in midst of divorce? exams?)
   Personal tastes (particularly in clothes, makeup)
   Habitual posture and gestures (clumsy? languid?)
   Personal habits (neat? frowsy? frazzled?)
5. Age (teeth or hair missing? child's facial structure?)
6. Physical peculiarities (hunchback, blindness, scars)
7. Objects habitually used or carried (lorgnette, leg-irons, cigar)
8. Resemblance to anybody (historical figure? some other character's grandfather?)
9. Period considerations
   Social class (Okie or heiress?)
   Sex (e.g., place of women at that time leading to habitual way of standing, glancing, moving, holding the head; see also social class)
   Upbringing and training (polo, military training, dancing, basketball, swordsmanship, horseback riding, tilting)
10. Style of the play (absurd? fantasy? classic Greek?)
11. Director's and designers' concepts

Study Projects

1. Go through a playscript and note down all clues to the visual image of one of the characters. Find clues in the dialogue, in the stage directions, or implied by your knowledge of the character's period and

environment. List your conclusions in one column and beside each one record the clue or clues that led you make that assessment.

2. Pick a character you like from any play. List ten sources outside the script for useful information about that character. Go personally to three of those sources (only one of them may be a book). Make notes and sketches of what you discover.

3. Begin a picture file by buying from a secondhand magazine shop three to six illustrated magazines, each in a different field. Clip pictures from your magazines that seem worth saving and decide on an appropriate subject category for each picture. (Note: The best category is the one that will allow you to retrieve the picture quickest when you need it.) Select enough pictures to make at least five categories. Label five folders or tabbed looseleaf pages with these categories. Arrange them alphabetically and file your pictures in them. Continue to collect material, making additional subject categories as you need them.

3

Designing a Facial Landscape

Drawing from Your Sources: What to Look For

Stimulated by the "givens" in the text and your research, fueled by overt or covert hints from director and designers, the imagination begins to take flight. Like the grain of sand in an oyster, these initial stimuli will continue to generate ideas and images until the finished pearl—a clear and unmistakable portrait of the character—is ready.

Knowing how and what to draw from your sources comes from an understanding of the actor's creative process. The first requisite is to give up all hope that the process is logical or linear. It is exactly the opposite: a hodgepodge of conflicting impressions that bombard the performer in such profusion that sorting them out, even if that were desirable, is a hopeless task.

The Impression Connection: Early Sightings

Gordon Craig described this early stage of the creative process perfectly. He was speaking as a stage designer but the actor's task is the same:

> I proceed in an illogical manner and try to perceive things feelingly, rather than thinkingly . . . I reach out and touch the play with my left hand, as it were, and try to receive the thing through my senses, and then make some note with my right hand which will record what it is I have felt. . . . Thinking comes afterwards. Thinking is for practical purposes. I think out a method of making clear to the spectator what I have felt and seen. (Gordon

Craig, quoted in *Directing the Play*, A Source Book of Stagecraft, ed. Toby Cole and Helen Chinoy [New York: Bobbs-Merrill, 1953], p. 45)

An impression, in this sense, is simply how something strikes you— "presses an imprint" (note figure 3). A picture, a piece of music, a stone wall, a play, the character, all send out quite specific signals. They telegraph a message of fast, slow, rough, heavy, light, agreeable or repugnant. They punch, tickle, stroke, block, stun. By seizing the pure and unexamined impression a character makes, the actor lays claim to ground on which the entire rest of the role will be constructed.

Children are masters at receiving and giving back uncensored impressions of the world around them.

> Brothers are big piles of dirt.
>   (Helena Clements, (P.S. 125)

> My heart feels like
> a porcupine
> with its sticky spikes and
> blood over them after it's
> just killed an animal

> When I sit by the shore
> watching a killer whale and
> it makes sounds,
> it sounds as if my mother was calling me.
>   (Jerome Wright, P.S. 28)

Children also know that the name by which a person or thing is commonly known may not begin to identify its true nature.

> A name like Wylie Eugene Fennell
> To me it sounds too intellectual
> It should be a name for a professor
> or an important person with class.
> To me, the name Stardust is like all
> of your imagination and mind. . . .
> like a star or a planet or something
> of outer space, like a hero, for all
> young people, a hero with style
> that leaves you breathless.
>   (Wylie Fennell, P.S. 125)

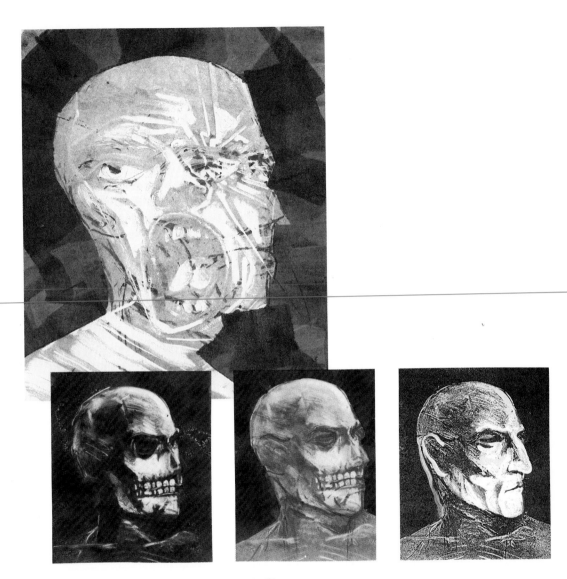

Fig. 3. Screaming Man by Reed Campbell.

When reaching for essences, literal descriptions are not always helpful.

> When I think of dance, the image of a prehistoric painting comes to mind. I see it drawn in the deepest and darkest place of a cave. (Ushio Amagatsu, director of the Sankai Juku dance troupe)

A favorite nonliteral impression is a student's description of Schnitzler's *La Ronde* as "a bowl of jello with different fruit in it. Every piece has its own shape and quality, but all the pieces are locked in the same environment." Another student saw the play as a "spiral staircase." A young actor's description of the turbulent barroom scene in *The Plough and the Stars*: "It's like a pinball machine." To his classmate, the scene was "a hive of buzzing bees or a bubbling stew in which Bessie Burgess is a rotten onion ready to burst." Costume draper Susan Davis describes the Furies in Cavalli's opera *La Calisto* as "a hit squad" wearing "killer earrings." Then there is Grotowski's description of life: "Daily life is for many people like an enormous restaurant or bar where everyone is just looking for drinks."

Energizing the Impression

Impressions are always highly personal. Asked for their impressions of the Saarinen Chapel, a bare, high-ceilinged room with an overhead skylight, participants in a theatre seminar came up with responses running all the way from "peaceful," "lyrical," and "serene" to "cold," "hospital," "frightening," and "star wars." Different individuals studying the same text pick out different details and make them central. The result is two different interpretations of the same role. Everyone's starting point, however, is identical: the text. Let us examine how the impressions garnered from the text give rise to the character image.

Here is a student's impression of The Little Miss from *La Ronde:* "She is like a flower that can close and open. When closed she is pink, but open the inside is bright red. She is very covered, lots of skirts, high-collared blouse, long sleeves, but she wears no underwear." Dostoevsky's metaphor for the German landlady, Amalia Ivanovna, in *Crime and Punishment* is an owl. Woyzeck's friend tells him, "You run through the world like a razor. . . . You're like a cow chased by a hornet." The heart of the metaphor is not the cow, of course, but the image of a driven, maddened, and therefore dangerous beast. Salvador Dali gave us Hamlet as a demonic Medusa spawning snakes that turn upon and consume their host.

Notice how the use of action verbs in the Woyzeck image brings the image to life. Try to express your impression of the character in active, dynamic terms: not "He is powerful," but "He sweeps the world to one side"; not "She is shy," but "She closes off from everyone."

Key impressions may be solid or fleeting, slow to arrive, or upon you with the speed of a striking snake. However they impact, each is a precious gift from the subconscious and, as we have said, provides the foundation upon which all subsequent refinements to the visual image will be made.

Working from the Key Impression

Let us suppose you wish to develop a makeup for the role of Elizabeth I of England. Let us further assume that someone has at last written a superb play about her latter days. You have read the script, started to collect pictures of the historic queen and her environment (fig. 4), and are alert to any clue to her character that observation can provide. The

Fig. 4. Elizabeth I, after a painting in the National Portrait Gallery (Reed Campbell).

problem is twofold: what to look for in your source material and how to translate what you see into a facial landscape. (You may choose any role you wish and work with it during the following discussion.) In order to illustrate working from impressions let us borrow Stella Adler's description of the aging Bess: "a mind surrounded by a graveyard."

Free Association as a First Step

Analyzing by free association the two parts of that impression might produce a list something like this:

Graveyard	*Mind*
Lurid	Head
Charnel house	Thinker
Francis Bacon's paintings	Insight
Grünewald's *Crucifixion*	Far-seeing
Burnt; ashes	Perceptive
Phantoms; haunted	Probing, darting, clever
Decay	Machiavellian, clever
Rotting, flies, maggots	Reason, rationality, wit
Lonely, forlorn, mourning	Judgment, command
Bones	Understanding
Debris	Mind over matter
Shroud	Strong-willed
Yellow, green, white	Genius
Earth colors	Brilliant
Dead or dying	*Wide awake, alive*

Notice that the last words mentioned are summaries and that the the summation carries the same dichotomy as the original impression: the shocking contrast inherent in juxtaposing "mind" and "graveyard." Now might be a good time to make a first quick thumbnail sketch of the character's face.

First Sketches: So You Think You Can't Draw

It is wise to record your initial impressions as soon as possible, not only in words, but with a rough sketch. Stifle the protests of your ego that you are incapable of producing a recognizable image of any living thing. It is totally unimportant whether your rendering is anatomically perfect. No one but you need ever see it; it is merely a shorthand notation of an image you have already constructed in your mind's eye. Think of it as a mental note you must jot down so that adjustments can be made to it as you would adjust a pattern or realign the pieces on a chessboard— more strengh here, a different direction there, better fit (fig. 5).

Fig. 5. Student initial-impression sketch by Robert Silver.

Examine your sketch. What has your right hand done with the information "perceived feelingly with your left," as Gordon Craig puts it, when you reached out and touched the role for the first time? Very likely it has instinctively borrowed from the traditional depiction of human facial extremes, the masks of comedy and tragedy. If the character is generally pleased with life, the muscles of the face will probably tend to hold firm or to pull very slightly upward. Age and depression will draw them down. A permanent or longstanding attitude of disgust, fear, suspicion, defiance, or any other "set" will similarly be reflected in subtle muscle tensions that clue the observer to the person's prevailing outlook, the attitude which has become part of the character's very substance. These are the signs that are picked up at first meetings between strangers. Their discreet presence in the makeup is the hallmark of a thoughtful and probing design.

Like other artists, performers do not work only from memory. Whatever models we require—the sharp, biting, lazy, frantic, or benign—can be found in nature, in the objects, flora, and fauna of this planet or in pictures of them.

Taking from Animals and Objects

How easy it would be if the perfect model for the character always turned out to be your mother's cousin or the manager of the local supermarket. Unfortunately, it is rare to see your character walking toward you, complete down to the last button. More likely, you will find a nose here, an eyebrow there and the rest of the face in various surprising places (fig. 6). Here is where a trip to the zoo or a museum or simply a brief tour of the neighborhood can be rewarding. This is also where a good picture file repays the time it took to assemble. You will not be the first to discover the amazing similarities between human and animal anatomies. Socrates believed men were reincarnated in birds and beasts with similar natures after death (fig. 7). "Those who have chosen the portion of injustice and tyranny and violence will pass into wolves, or into hawks and kites—whither else can we suppose them to go?" (Plato, *Phaedo*).

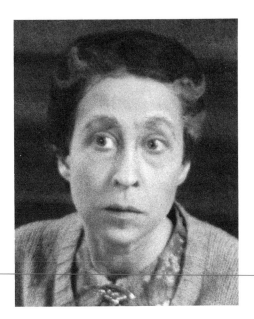

Fig. 6. A townswoman in Carson McCullers's *Ballad of the Sad Café*.

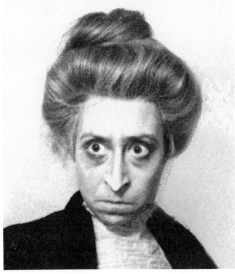

Fig. 7. Actress as Mrs. Gogan in *The Plough and the Stars* by Sean O'Casey.

What Mourns in Nature?

From our free association list for Elizabeth I, let's select the most evocative, visually suggestive words and see what they bring to mind. A good way of finding an object to draw from is to ask questions. What darts? Insects dart. What is it to be strong-willed? It is to be immovable—like a rock. What mourns in nature? The drooping branches of a willow.

To draw an impression from a picture, an animal, a piece of furniture, ask yourself "What does it do most?" A Louis V chair might squat, a porcupine bristles. You are using the chair for your makeup concept, not because it is eighteenth century, but because it squats, and the florid cheeks of your character, George III, will squat on your face (fig. 8).

Continuing to free-associate for our Elizabeth I makeup, we find connections between impressions and recall relevant objects that we may have seen in other contexts. We can begin to decide where in the face of the queen they will find a place.

Fig. 8. Louis XV chair; George III, after a caricature by James Gillray, 1792 (Reed Campbell).

Impressions of Elizabeth I	Where Found	Where Used
Lurid, burnt, ashes	Old campsite	Skin color
Bones	A skeleton	Prominent bones
Rotting	Grünewald Christ	Complexion texture
Mourning	A willow tree	Sagging flesh
Mind	A skull	Large, bared skull
Farseeing, probes, darts	Insect eye	Brow and eyes
Strong-willed	A rock	Set of the mouth
		Aquiline nose

Find what it is about the Grünewald Christ that suggests to you corruption. The greenish pallor of the corpse? The bruised and decomposing flesh? Take what you want for your image and put it where you want it on your sketch. "Bones." Shall their unfleshed bareness be expressed in a jutting, angular chin (fig. 9a), or will you emphasize it in the domelike forehead (fig. 9b)? What mourns in the sovereign's face? Shall the eyebrows droop like willow branches, or the flesh sag from the bones in flaccid folds (fig. 9c), or both?

Examine the picture of the insect you have selected. Decide whether it is the bulging eye or the arching carapace above it that best bespeaks the piercing glance, the watchful, all-seeing gaze of the old queen. Steal the detail you need and incorporate it into the sketch. Perhaps by now you have dispensed with pencil and paper and are trying all this out on a face that is becoming more and more unlike the one you were born with (fig. 9d). Like a rock, Elizabeth stood firm against all challengers. Now, after sixty years, the hardness shows in the chiseled, aquiline nose and thin, sharp mouth (fig. 9e, f). For completed makeup, see figure 11.

Sharp-focusing the Character Image

As you learn more about the character, its features will alter, much as they would in a police sketch, until idea and execution match. Even slight changes to a feature can make a big difference. The proverbial example of this is Cleopatra's nose which, had it been a smidgin shorter or longer would, we are told, have altered the course of the Roman Empire! Below are two good approaches to developing the characterization in makeup.

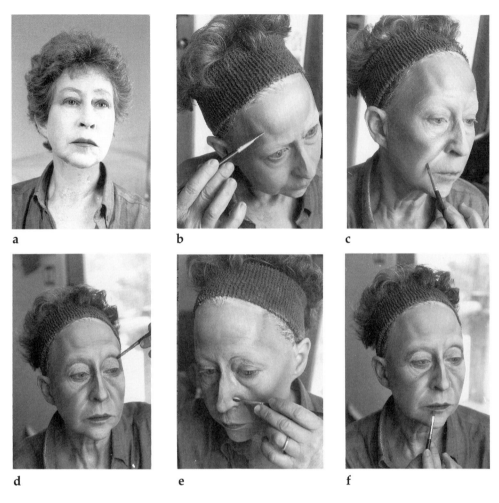

Fig. 9. Elizabeth I makeup: *(a)* Prior to application, *(b)* forehead, *(c)* cheek fold, *(d)* eye ridge, *(e)* nose, *(f)* mouth.

Emphasizing a Major Feature

When you have achieved a fairly clear image of the character, you may want to call attention to features that emphasize a particular character trait, i.e., a strong chin, an inquisitive nose, large doelike eyes. Even minor adjustments to the features are immediately apparent at a distance of a few feet, but small changes do not carry far and tend to be washed out by strong light. You will need to emphasize what you want to be seen by all parts of the house, and those features that most strongly define the character. Often, one feature can provide a focus for the whole makeup: Jimmy Durante's nose, Whoopi Goldberg's hairdo are cases in point. (Cartoonists shorten the time it takes to perceive character by using this method and the one discussed below. Be careful with these two powerful tools if you wish to avoid caricature.)

Asymmetry: Unruly Nature, Cruel Time

Most people are born with one eye slightly larger than the other, one eyebrow higher than its mate. Usually we take pains to disguise the discrepancy, but in the theatre the opposite may sometimes be our aim. Alec Guinness, although avowedly a believer in less, rather than more, makeup created a brilliant face for his Richard III by making use of asymmetry to suggest tricky Dicky's slyness and double-dealing (fig. 10). Age, of course, will distort the most regular features (see chapter 13).

Fig. 10. Alec Guinness as Richard III (Reed Campbell).

The Decision to Use Plastic Constructions

You may find that the changes you wish to make are so far-reaching that your own features cannot be made to simulate convincingly the ones you have elected for the character. At this point, you may wish to turn to plastic, latex, or gauze constructions called prostheses. Don't be too quick, however, to assume the case is hopeless without artificial aids. First try what subtle blending and clever design can do, testing the result before someone you trust to tell you if it will pass audience inspection. As a rule, when derma wax drops off of its own weight, or gauze will not hold because the flesh beneath it is too mobile, the time has come for a carefully constructed prosthesis. Some of these can be fabricated by the actor or bought ready-made. Others require technical expertise beyond the range of most performers (see chapter 12).

Study Projects

1. Collect or take from your picture file two pictures that you think are interesting for character. Bring them to class and exchange impressions with your fellow students. Try to express your impressions in active verbs. Not "I like this, it's colorful," but "This stabs!" or "The snow in that picture is smothering the flowers."

2. Rename yourself or a classmate with a name that describes what or who that individual is. Have fun, but be helpful, not harmful.

3. Examine a character you might play. From a careful reading of the script, form an impression of that character and describe him or her, using the most active and evocative language you can. Free-associate from your impression to find additional terms that suggest various aspects of the character.

4. Think of someone you know. Select an animal that person reminds you of and list the features they share in common. Do a caricature sketch or cartoon of that person as the animal you have selected.

5. Make a cartoon drawing of someone you know or of yourself, emphasizing those features that are most typical of that person. Make use of asymmetry.

4

Crown to Toe: Extensions of the Face Makeup

Interdependence of Face and Body

Whatever the audience can see is the domain of makeup, whether it is glimpsed for an instant only or subjected to prolonged scrutiny. During the final week of rehearsals for a Circle-in-the-Square production of *Desire under the Elms,* a hurry call went out for a makeup expert. Assistance was needed for making up the back of George C. Scott's neck—specifically, the gap between hairline and collar. It was not clear if the actor was unable to reach the desired spot himself, or whether suddenly faced, so to speak, with the back of his neck in the makeup mirror, he was bemused to the point of paralysis. Whatever the case, Mr. Scott had clearly determined that no visible part of his anatomy should fail to reflect the character of Ephraim Cabot.

His thoroughness points up the total interdependence of face and body. The hipbone is most assuredly connected to the thighbone. To disengage one part from another is to destroy the integrity of the organism. Alter the tilt of the head and the line of the neck is changed. Hunch the shoulders and the result is a double chin (see chapter 18).

An actress still shy of middle age created the role of the oceangoing Old Woman in Edward Albee's *Box-Mao-Box.* At rise, she was discovered far downstage, one clawlike hand poised on the ship's rail. Its skinny index finger moved imperceptibly, tapping out the impatience which was soon to give rise to an outburst of speech that would establish at one fell swoop her character, emotional state, and intention. The actress' hands were small and pudgy. Had she not made them up with as much care and thought as she had given her face, the credibility of the character would have been shattered before she had opened her mouth. This attention to outlying areas extends even to the choice of costume elements and props, as we shall see later. The first and most obvious extension of the facial features, however, is hair.

Hair: Pivotal Resource for Change

Mélisande is at the window in one of the towers of the castle, combing her unbound hair, as she speaks to Pélléas below:

>My long locks fall foaming
>> To the threshold of the tower.
>My locks await your coming
>> All along the tower
>> And all the long, long hour.

Pélléas: thy locks. . . .
>They are alive like birds in my hands. . . . and
>they love me, they love me more than you do!

Not all coiffures are as pivotal to the play as Mélisande's, but it is obvious from the many comments people receive who have just changed their hairstyle how much hair contributes to overall appearance. Hairstyling is the quick-change artist's ace in the hole. No other alteration makes such a radical difference in the appearance of the character as does a change of coiffure or the addition of a beard or mustache. Spy novelists know this; false hair is always the villain's first recourse when disguise is needed. It conceals not only identity but weak chins, overly short or long upper lips, and whatever the wearer may be thinking. Facial hair can add age or hide it, broaden faces or thin them, read suave, sage, or scruffy, depending on its shape and color. It can make you look taller and camouflage unduly prominent ears or a high forehead. As for eyebrows, the writer knows an actress who will not allow a makeup artist to touch them. She maintains that more character resides in the shape of an eyebrow than anywhere else in the face.

For these reasons, hair shape, color, and style should be selected with the utmost care and never merely on the basis of what is "period." In any period there are dozens of correct hairstyles, but only one that is perfect for the character (see chapter 15).

Costume Elements as Extensions of the Makeup

Choosing a personal prop or an element of costume is a crucial step in the process of developing a role and is obviously a highly individual matter. No two actors will "dress" the part in quite the same way, but the goal of their effort is the same: clothing and props should help the actor to play the part and the audience to grasp the character's essence and relation to the play. For this, the cooperation of the designer must be sought, as it was when a promising young actress took over the role of a brothelkeeper in a long-running off-Broadway musical.

The actress' predecessor in the part was a sensuous creature with a vibrant personality and the voice of a Bette Midler. She needed no help to project a madam, and her costume gave her none. Her replacement, on the other hand, was small in stature and felt rather unsuited to the role. She asked for and received from the understanding designer a completely new costume, revealing where the original had covered, flashy where the other had been drab. A wisp of boa was amplified for her into an explosion of feathers from which her chest, also somewhat amplified, could project like a pouter pigeon's. Finally, lacking the wild mane of hair that the first actress had worn au naturel, actress number two secured a frizzed cap of bleached blond ringlets.

Not all designers are so obliging. As artists, they are naturally eager to preserve the integrity of their creations. To some, this means retention of the flavor, permitting alteration of details that can be changed without loss to the original concept. To others, it means holding fast to every buckle, button, and bow.

By contrast, there are designers who will practically allow the actor to design his own costume. William Ritman was one of these, and one time escorted the writer to a Salvation Army depot where together they spent hours poring through the racks, pulling garments until both designer and player were satisfied. The memory is still fresh of Bill emptying four oil drums of galoshes to find the mate to the one they had both recognized instantly as perfect for the character. Another time in Boston, however, she was met with blank noncomprehension by a different designer when, taking over the role of the hunchback Jeanne from the ailing Anne Bancroft in *The Devils,* she requested a hump that was a bit off to one side rather than patly centered.

Unfortunately, there are no set rules on how to deal with fellow artists when disagreements arise. Rational discussion usually results in a satisfactory compromise. If it does not, what are the options? If you're small potatoes, you will be conciliatory and beg. If you have weight, you can try throwing it around, but only as a last resort. If you simply cannot STAND that mauve dressing gown with the frangipani that they have given you for the third act and use it to wipe the radiators, you must be willing to accept the consequences of your action. As in all matters concerned with the production, the director has the final say.

Like the prosthesis and facial hair, costume elements can be used to camouflage and to complete the image of the character. A scrawny neck can be veiled with a shawl, a double chin masked by a high collar. Notice in figure 11 how the addition of costume elements and props completes the makeup for Queen Elizabeth and carries through the character image.

Personal Props: An Actor's Choices

The concern for the hinter regions of a makeup that is natural to the professional extends to the actor's choice of personal props that provide visible and sometimes audible clues to the character. At the end of the Broadway premiere production of *The Ballad of the Sad Café,* a townswoman's offer of friendship was brusquely rejected by the main character, who demanded her money instead. There was a long hesitation; then a single sound abruptly cut the silence—the dry snap of the woman's purse as she closed it with finality, taking both money and friendship with her in a rapid exit. When the play was being dressed, several bags were tested by the actress before she found one with just the right "if that's the way you want it" click. For this actress, the audience's understanding of her character depended as much on her choice of a reticule as on the hollows in her cheeks or the way she arranged her hair. To have left any of these decisions entirely up to others would have seemed to her an abdica-

Fig. 11. Finished makeup for Elizabeth I. Photograph by William
McGonigle, costume courtesy the Santa Fe Opera.

tion of her responsibility for the role. Such care does not go unnoticed. A review treasured by the writer was one in which her baggy lisle stockings received equal praise with her performance.

At rehearsals for the premiere of Jack Gelber's *Cuban Thing*, the writer remembers watching with interest the metamorphosis of a handkerchief worn by cast member Michael Wager. In act 1 it was a banner of conspicuous proportions, flamboyantly displayed. At the play's end, a different handkerchief, soberly squared and flattened, barely showed above the jacket pocket. Mindy's explanation: "Everything is toned down with him now." And indeed the character appeared depressed, deflated, emptied of all vitality.

In the Hogarth engravings *A Rake's Progress*, a hairdresser is shown busily preparing curling papers for the mistress of the house. Tucked behind his ear is a comb, symbol of his trade and a constant tool (fig. 12).

Fig. 12. A hairdresser, after Hogarth (Reed Campbell).

For an actor, the decision to "wear" that comb represents a choice as crucial to the visual image as the choice of wig style or nose shape. Personal props such as these may legitimately be requested by the actor and even obtained or made by him or her after consultation with the director and designer. (See also chapter 20.)

Study Projects

1. Stand in profile before a full-length mirror. Round your shoulders and thrust out your stomach. Notice what effect this has on your jaw and the angle at which your head attaches to your neck. Hunch your shoulders and tuck your chin in. Notice the number of chins this adds to the one you have.

2. Study paintings or photographs of people from three different periods. Sit or stand in front of the mirror and copy the pose of the person in the picture. How does it change your neck? your eyes? In what part of your face do you feel a difference? Is the skin drawn more tautly over your cheekbones? Are your eyes more heavy-lidded or more alert than usual?

3. Choose a character from a play. If you have no access to wigs or to ready-made beards and mustaches, select a style of coiffure or a style of facial hair for the character and simulate it with yarn, false hair, or even paper. Hold it in place with adhesive tape or wire. See how the hair changes the shape of your face. Does it make you look older? younger? taller?

4. Add a hat, collar, and jewelry appropriate to the period. If a costume collection is not available, simulate these with paper, cardboard, or scraps of fabric. Add one personal prop the character would use. Walk around in character. Notice how the costume and prop elements affect the way you move, hold your head, the set of your features, the way you feel.

5

Nationality: Legitimate Concept or Baseless Fiction?

Is There a National Image to Convey?

Lorca authority Gwynne Edwards speaks of Federico Garcia Lorca as a writer whose "Spanishness never obscures the universality of his work." Paradoxically, he says, that universality can only be realized fully in performance through a firm grasp of the writer's "Spanishness." Can one lay claim, by birth or background, to a detectable difference between oneself and others, and is this difference significant to the performer?

A standard reference book on foreign dialects begins each chapter with a description characterizing a particular nationality. Under "Spanish dialect" we read: "The Spaniard is perhaps the personification of the so-called Latin temperament. The heated blood, the fiery eye, the impassioned speech, the volatile temper, the colorful idiom, the sensuous music, the poetic expression—all these are typical of the Spanish psyche." There are specific directives on inflection and pitch:"The pitch in such emotional people," the author says, "would naturally be much higher than in American." Finally, we are assured that the Spaniard is at once "hot-headed, sentimental, lazy," and "an impassioned lover of the beautiful."

Modern sociology rejects such confident generalizations, replacing them with cautious references to the effects of climate, topography, and tradition on national character. Agreement about ethnic distinctions has never been easy to obtain, for even at a time when opinions were boldly offered as fact, during the early to mid-twentieth century, every statement evoked its opposite:

That the Spanish woman is passionate goes without saying.[1]	She is chaste and dispassionate."[2]
The Spaniard is a shrewd businessman.[3]	The Spaniard . . . always is and perhaps always will be essentially un-businesslike.[4]
The character of the Spanish temperament (is) . . . marked not by classic feeling—but by the romantic spirit.[5]	The Spaniards are, as a rule, matter-of-fact, and infinitely less romantic than English spinsters.[6]

One must acknowledge the difficulty of separating fact from fiction. At the same time, it is possible to recall numerous *Bernarda Alba* productions that failed because the actresses looked like American teeny-boppers. If there is truth in the concept of "nationality," where does it lie and how is the actor in search of a character image to distinguish it from falsehood and cliché? Is the woman tasting tomato sauce in the TV commercial "That's Italian!" representative of anyone or anything to which an audience can relate?

Maria Benitez, internationally recognized dancer and choreographer (fig. 13), has been called "a veritable volcano" who conveys "not simply physical sensation, but a series of almost unnameable moods—from dark to dazzling." *New York Magazine* says of her, "she inhabits her dances so fully she seems to go on a journey to another place, taking the viewer with her . . . a capability that only great dancers share. . . . Benitez per-

1. Louis Higgin, *Spanish Life in Town and Country* (New York: G. P. Putnam and Sons, 1902), 54.
2. Waldo Frank, *Virgin Spain* (London: Jonathan Cape, 1952), 245.
3. André Siegfried, *The Character of Peoples* (London: Jonathan Cape, 1952), 40.
4. Havelock Ellis, *The Soul of Spain* (Boston: Houghton Mifflin, n.d.), 11.
5. Ellis, 20.
6. Mario Praz, *Unromantic Spain* (New York: Alfred A. Knopf, 1929), 16.

Fig. 13. Maria Benitez and partner. Photograph by by Ken Howard, courtesy the Institute for Spanish Arts.

forming Flamenco is akin to the Martha Graham of Clytemnestra and to Ulanova as the Dying Swan." And yet, this foremost exponent of a quintessentially Spanish dance form was born in Minnesota to a Native American Indian mother and a Puerto Rican father, studied initially to be a ballet dancer, and saw Spain for the first time as a young woman. During a recent interview with the writer, Maria Benitez discussed the origin and significance of national differences:

JE: An authority on Lorca speaks of that writer's "Spanishness." Is there such a thing, and if so, how would you define it?

MB: Spanish arts, Spanish dance in particular, is of a certain temperament . . . it has tremendous profoundity and in many ways it's extremely introverted and stoic. Another characteristic is uninhibitedness, which is very difficult for, say, Americans to demonstrate. Spaniards are quick to anger, quick to laugh . . . very quick to anger and very emotional, but it's over with in a minute. For me, Spanish dance, particularly flamenco, has all of those emotions of . . . tenderness, want, agression, earthiness, elegance, refinement . . . anger, love, coquettishness. All of those elements are in the dance and all of those elements are usually in our personalities.

Spanishness is also very tragic. By the same token that they are one of the most lively people, they're also very much prone to live for the moment, especially flamenco people—to express the moment, and "tomorrow I will die." A lot of us say "You will die, and *you* will die and you will die but *I* will *never* die. Spaniards don't think that way at all. They confront death much easier than other people do; in fact, sometimes they get a little too obsessed with it.

JE: Where does "Spanishness" come from—family background, climate, geography, history?

MB: I think it's from the history, from the religious mores, the Spanish Inquisition . . . a tremendous cruelty. You look at the bullfight. This, for most Spaniards, is a celebration and for most Americans it's just a . . . well, the Humane Society should be moving in and putting these people into jail, or something!

The fact that women were not allowed to wear slacks. . . . I remember the 1960s in Spain, you were not allowed to show any affection openly in public. Girls who went out had to be chaperoned. In the theatre, you could not show your midriff; it had to have a piece of hose on it, that kind of thing. . . . But what I found really interesting was that you turn right around and you have one of the most sensual and possibly one of the most erotic art forms which is their dance. It was always rather incongrous to me. I mean, you would expect stately court dances and that kind of thing. They found another way of being able to let that emotional energy out, and this is also why flamenco was considered very low-class. Only the low-class people did this kind of thing and the rich people would go and see them. It was compared to the blues and jazz. . . . But it was especially interesting to me that this very sensual art form could come out of such a tight, rigid society. I guess that is the reason why they did have these other outlets. The bullfight is another outlet for the emotions and for pent-up energy. Their robust outgoingness, I think, is another way that they are able to let energy out, because the other channels were certainly very much closed off to them.

JE: Do you believe we should deemphasize national differences so that people may be more alike, or are ethnic distinctions valuable and should we preserve them?

MB: Oh, I think they're very valuable, and I think we should start preserving them, very much so. I would hate to see everybody the same. How bloody boring! And I think we learn so much from other ethnic groups as to what is their sense of beauty, what is their sense of time, what is their sense of tradition, and how does it differ from ours. Maybe we don't agree with it, but we have to open ourselves at least to understand that it exists and accept it on those terms. It doesn't mean that we're going to run to the nearest gypsy camp and live with a bunch of gypsies, but to understand who they are and how they function, how they differ from us, what is acceptable to them, and what is not acceptable, and why—I think that's important.

You take the American Indian (I take these groups because I know at least something about them). In many ways they're an extremely introverted people, but I also found them very giving—and very private, the opposite of what Spaniards are. I think what strikes me most is their ability to see beyond themselves.

JE: See to what?

MB: The things of nature. Little, simple things bring them great joy. . . . I think the Indian also is not ego-oriented. It's not "Me, I, that have to go out and be the best." They have a sense of "We will ALL be . . . we will all work together," which is totally the opposite of anything in Spanish dance or flamenco that you could possibly think of.

JE: Is it possible for a non-Hispanic to play a Hispanic? How could he or she prepare for the role?

MB: First of all, you have to have a tremendous self-security. One of my main doubts when I first got into Spanish dance was "But I'm not Spanish. Do I have the emotion to do this?" And to this day, I still get comments from Spaniards like "She dances very well for not being a Spaniard." In fact, it's become a standing joke—I'm the first one to say it. It doesn't bother me anymore because I'm secure with what I do and I have told them myself, "My blood is just as red as yours, if not redder!"

You do have to immerse yourself in the culture. I think you'd have to be a real phenomenon to be able to perform, say, flamenco, without ever having been to Spain. . . . You have to understand where some of the things were born—why they exist. You have to be able to see kids dancing flamenco in the street. You have to see the old ladies get up and dance in the street. You have to see flamenco that's raw, gutsy power at four in the morning after four bottles of wine—those things you have to experience to understand what it is.

JE: You seem to be suggesting that if you do observe the culture and immerse yourself in it, that it's possible that a person who's not Hispanic could have the same emotional resources inside to—

MB: Definitely!

JE: In other words, it's there, and by studying the culture and being able to draw from yourself, that no person is barred from—

MB: Absolutely not.

JE: Playing an Italian, a Hispanic, an Indian, an Afghanistani, a Soviet Russian—

MB: Right, absolutely right. . . . To become acquainted with another culture and understand it a little bit and move with it and feel with it—I think all those things are very much a help.

When Ethnic Distinctions Are Helpful

Certainly, simplistic notions about racial identity will no longer hold water. Societies today are highly mobile. Two world wars, numerous "police actions" around the globe, the breakdown of traditional antipathy to mixed marriages, the speed of air travel, have all contibuted to the disappearance of racial boundaries and to discrediting the concept of race itself.

Many plays, however, depend on ethnic distinctions and take meaning from the friction between characters who see each other as physically unlike. *Othello* is a classic example of this type of play. Although black and white actors frequently interchange the roles of Iago and Othello, the effect on Desdemona's father of the line "an old black ram / is tupping your white ewe," symbolic as it is of the deep-rooted feelings of many in the white society of that time and place, cannot be vitiated without breaking the play's back. The blackness of Tituba in *The Crucible* and Clay in Baraka's *Dutchman* are likewise pivotal to the playwrights' themes. In *Marco Polo, West Side Story,* Robinson Jeffers's *Medea, Royal Hunt of the Sun, Mr. Harold and the Boys,* and *Driving Miss Daisy,* it is precisely this confrontation of people alien to each other that sparks the drama. Their mutual distrust or attraction stems partly from the physical differences between them, and these differences can be made substantive by makeup.

To repeat, it is how these people perceive each other and how they are perceived by the audience that thoughtful use of makeup can reinforce. Only when the rendering lacks subtlety and the bounds of realism and good taste are exceeded is the result cliché or caricature. (For a discussion of caricature see chapter 6. For a chart of ethnic distinctions, see plate 1, appendix A, and for discussion of application, see chapter 17.)

Study Projects

1. Choose a character of a different ethnic background than yours (an Inca, a Chinese, a Native American, a Scandinavian, a North African). Begin to research the character's environment, personality, life history, in preparation for doing a makeup as that character in chapter 17.

2. Visit a neighborhood where people of a particular nationality or ethnic background live or work in large numbers. Make notes on physical and temperamental characteristics that seem typical or widespread.

6

Beyond Naturalism: Stylized Makeups

How was it possible, one wonders, that actors rehearsing for the premiere productions of Ionesco and Arrabal in this country could have been so at sea? But we were, and since no one seemed able to elucidate the bizarre dialogue, we coped with it as best we could, suspecting that had we recited from the Dow Jones Report, the effect would have been much the same. Between the 1920s plays of Apollinaire, Artaud, and Tzara and the 1950s there had been little opportunity to experience the theatre of the absurd. "Serious" actors were preoccupied with the earnest social realism of O'Casey, Odets, and Elmer Rice, in whose plays they practiced the methods of in-depth psychological characterization popularized by the Group Theatre. Nothing prepared performers who were fledging their wings in the 1950s and 1960s for the imminent overturn of many of their long-held theories about what consituted proper acting technique and play structure.

American playwrights seemed to cotton to the absurd more quickly than actors and directors. Long after absurdist plays had begun to appear on Broadway there was still widespread bafflement about how to approach them in performance. Years after Albee's *Box-Mao-Box* debuted in Buffalo, Ruth White and the author of this book were comparing notes one day and found, with little surprise, that our frantic queries on the meaning of a line or even of whole scenes had often received answers from both playwright and director that were too vague to be of use.[1]

Even the incomparable Bert Lahr confessed to bewilderment when first confronted with *Godot* and ended up relying heavily on doing what came naturally.

Heightened and Slanted Characters

While many foundered in confusion, Stella Adler was formulating rules of deportment for the world of fantasy. Her concepts of heightened and slanted characterization and her explanation of caricature gave guidance to generations of young actors making the transition from *Waiting for Lefty* to *Waiting for Godot, Cats,* and *Starlight Express.*

Adler drew a distinction between characters that were mildly eccentric—those that, although exaggerated or "heightened," could nevertheless be seen walking on the street—and characters that were full-scale excursions into the unreal. The first are distorted as far as nature will permit. The last are distorted beyond the limits of the waking world and belong to the outer reaches, the realm of dreams, nightmares, mystic visions, and the hallucinations of the insane.

Distinctions among Comedy, Farce, Satire, and Fantasy

Comedy, farce, and satire can all be hosts to the fantastic. Comic characters are frequently heightened; examples are Lady Bracknell, Malvolio, Tartuffe, and the charwomen created by Carol Burnett and Lily Tomlin. Farce, which might be described as comedy gone bananas, lets the heightening shade into caricature, producing the half-men-half-beasts of *Rhinoceros,* the Muppets' Swedish cook, wrestler "Gorgeous George" and his derivatives, "Crazy Eddie"—that prototype of television huckster-ism gone round the bend—and the wacky creations of Charles Ludlam's theatre of the ridiculous. In comedy and farce, ridicule tends to remain

1. Ten years later, while the present writer was preparing to be a guest panelist in a symposium on Albee, the whole play suddenly seemed crystal clear. *Box,* with its image of "one bird flying in the opposite direction," is surely one of the most poignant metaphors ever conceived for our perturbed society.

lighthearted and entertainment is usually the main objective. Satire results from the infusion of strong political or social overtones, as in *Candide* and *Mastergate*. Satire has a cutting edge that gives it "bite" and turns its wit and whimsy slightly acid. Often, it presents a character from a particular person's slant, i.e., an environmentalist as seen by the head of a strip-mining company or an American as seen through the eyes of a Calcutta beggar. The trolls in Mark Lamos's production of *Peer Gynt* are another example—bestial, spike-haired takeoffs on the punk-rock generation.

All three forms give the performer liberty to pull the visual image out of normal proportion, emphasizing some features and eliminating others, making things much too large or much too small. (As an example, see figure 14.) The effect is very much like that of a supermarket mirror that gives a view of the store not as it appears in life but stretched, broadened, or narrowed in one or more of its dimensions. Fantasy results when the boundaries of everyday reality are totally overstepped and we are through the looking glass hobnobbing with trolls, demons, faeries, and talking dogs.

a   b

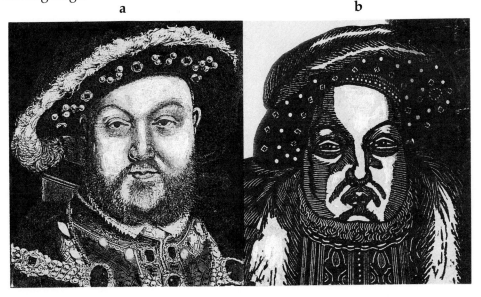

Fig. 14. Henry VIII: *(a)* after Holbein (Reed Campbell); *(b)* sixteenth-century woodcut; after an original in the Pierpont Morgan Library.

The World of Fantasy

To reach fantasy, the normally logical mind does a broad jump that lands it in a world ruled by discontinuity and surprise. There, the intellect foregoes its attachment to linear thought—three apples and two apples make five apples—and arrives by daredevil leaps and bounds at improbable conclusions. In the world of fantasy, three apples and two apples can be a bag of diamonds, an army of ten thousand, or a dinner of cheese. Children and the insane are equally at home with fantasy because their inner logic travels a highly personal path from *A* to *Z*. Its twists and turns are clear to them but appear to others devious and obscure. Unexpected connections are made instantaneously and as quickly converted into action. This coincidence of thought and action applies to the creation of the visual image. In fantasy, "He is like a spider" becomes "He *is* a spider."

Borrowing from Natural Forms

The example is apt, for throughout history, models for phantasmagoric images have been taken from the natural world. Various forms of animal and plant life, sometimes incorporated with inanimate objects, are either superimposed on, or amalgamated with, the human physiognomy, as shown in figures 15 and 16. (And see also figure 23. To achieve the startling similarity of Death [a] to an owlet [b], the maskmaker stretched and distorted white rubber to convey the effect of a lurid creature of the night.)

When designing a phantasmagoric image, facial contours should not be changed capriciously. Alterations work best when they are natural extensions of human forms and functions. For example, Hieronymous Bosch will elongate the noses of his medieval demons until they become trumpets out of which noxious fumes are blown, and extend the jaw of a glutton into a pig's snout. Both are logical exaggerations of the original feature's shape and purpose. The mask and costume for "Fire" in figure 17 makes flamelike extensions of every limb and feature. Use the method outlined in chapter 3 for drawing impressions from pictures or actual objects and incorporating them into a fantastic makeup.

Fig. 15. Boar, painted wood. Patamban, Michoacán, Mexico, ca. 1960. Courtesy Museum of International Folk Art.

Fig. 16. Mouse, painted wood. Made by Estaneslado Pablo y Gomez. Xalpatlahuac, Guerrero, Mexico, ca. 1975. Courtesy Museum of International Folk Art.

Fig. 17. Rita Shane as "Fire" in *l'Enfant et les Sortilèges*.
Photograph by Martin Weil, courtesy the Santa Fe Opera.

Masked Characters: Instant Other

Freedoms and Constraints

It is in the course of designing a nonnaturalistic makeup that the need is most likely to arise for masks and mask makeups. Masks have existed for at least 17,000 years. The mask is the archetype of all makeups. It is the easiest means of achieving "instant other." Underneath it, the "I" can be totally concealed and "him," "her," or "it" fully disclosed or withdrawn in favor of a neutrality of feature that allows the actor maximum freedom.

Freedom and constraint are the twin attributes of masks. Libby Appel notes "the tremendous safety behind the mask. . . . The masked actor represents someone other than himself, and this anonymity produces a miraculous sensation of freedom. With the mask acting as a 'permission-giver,' the actor can do anything, be anyone. He can plumb deep into his resources and tap his soul, imagination, and experiences. By covering, the actor uncovers."[2]

But the freedom is not boundless. Constraint comes from the subservience of the actor to the mask's demands. Except for neutral, expressionless masks, its fixed expression, like Macbeth's dagger, marshals the performer the way that he must go. It is guide, dictator, and constant companion every moment the actor is onstage.

Designing a Mask or Mask Makeup

For this reason, the actor needs to think through the character he wishes to convey and distill its essence carefully into the features of the mask, for those features will not be subject to alteration. To paraphrase the De Beers ad, "A mask is forever." A mask may be an intensification of a single attitude or emotion like rage or grief, or it may be an abstraction of an ethnic image or chronological age (fig. 18).

Masks have been used to hide identity, to protect, frighten, or control; to impersonate someone or something; to empower the wearer and give license to insult or even to kill; to teach, amuse, or entertain;

2. Libby Appel, *Mask Characterization: An Actor's Process* (Carbondale: Southern Illinois University Press, 1982), xiv.

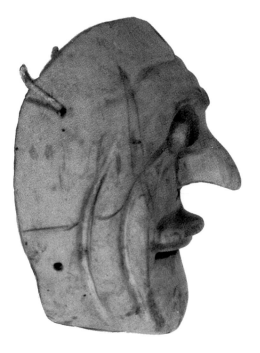

Fig. 18. Old man, unpainted wood. Michoacán, Mexico, ca. 1940. Courtesy Museum of International Folk Art.

to hide disfigurement; or to represent what is too horrible to show explicitly. They are a natural means of creating caricatures in satire (figs. 19, 20, and 21).

Symbolic Meaning

Their effect depends on a collective understanding of their meaning by the group watching, and so the symbolism of the colors, shapes, and materials used in their fabrication must be clear to the audience members. Masks are designed to be "read" over distance, instantly, like a billboard and therefore tend to be boldly drawn and greatly simplified. Insignificant details drop away and important features are exaggerated, as they are in heightened character.

Suprahuman Characters and Archetypes

A mask is seldom merely a human face. It must say more than the naked face could, or there would be no need for it (as can be seen in figure 22). It is also the true test of an actor's willingness to subordinate his

Fig. 19. Rue McClanahan and James Antonio in *The Raree Show,*
Four Winds Theatre live documentary performed at the American
Museum in Britain. Photograph by William McGonigle.

Fig. 20. James Doing in *The Nose* by Dmitry Shostakovich. Photograph by Murrae Haynes, courtesy the Santa Fe Opera.

Fig. 22. Viejito, lacquered wood
with glass eyes. Uruapan,
Michoacán, Mexico, ca. 1920.
Courtesy Museum of Inter-
national Folk Art.

Fig. 21. Man with cigar, painted wood.
Atlixtac, Guerrero, Mexico, ca. 1965.
Gift of Kathleen and Robert Kaupp,
courtesy Museum of International
Folk Art.

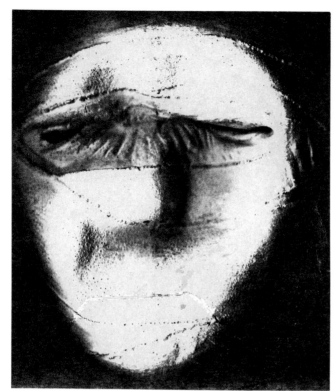

a

b

Fig. 23. Mask of Death (a),
Baby owl (b); used in Moon, Take
My Face, documentary on
Ethiopia. Borough of Manhattan
Community College.

Fig. 24. Mask of Satan, designed by Mosca for *The Hegge-Wakefield Nativity,* as seen on public television, New York. (Choreography by Mary Anthony.) Photograph by Alan Haas.

personal identity to the part. An actor once refused a leading role in a play the writer was directing solely because the character was masked, and he was afraid agents wouldn't know who he was. Mummenschantz actress Pilar Garcia speaks of the need to get the actor's personality out of the way: "Your job is to fulfill the mask."

As has been said, one of the problems with stylized makeups is that they depend on audience recognition of the intention behind the manipulation of an image. In order to satirize something, the thing that is being singled out for mockery or special note must be familiar in its original form. It must be part of a common tradition, a matter of common knowledge, before any change worked upon it can be funny or meaningful. Modern cartoonists complain that it is hard to find images now to which all people respond, because much that was known by people of average education is no longer taught in the schools, and because our population contains so many diverse cultures. Archetypes, which depend heavily on group tradition, are especially hard to come by. Probably one of the few archetypes familiar to all Americans today is Mickey Mouse. The devil, or Satan, is another archetype whose symbolic representation is fairly well defined. Customarily, he is portrayed (fig. 24) as a sardonic, savage, half animal, complete with claws, fangs, and mane of coarse hair. (See chapter 19, which discusses the design and fabrication of masks.)

Study Projects

1. Design a makeup for Ariel or Caliban in *The Tempest*. Make an initial sketch from your impressions of the role, refining it as you discover more about the character. Make a separate sketch for each revision. It is interesting and instructive to see how the character image develops and what changes it undergoes in the process.

2. Choose a character from fantasy. It can be from a children's book, an Elizabethan play, a modern fantasy, or science fiction. Design a mask or mask makeup for the character that incorporates elements from the plant or animal world. If possible, do the sketch in color. Indicate how the mask is to be made, what materials you would use, and how any technical problems such as weight, eye or mouth mobility, or quick changes would be solved.

7

Makeup for
Special Circumstances

When there is great distance between viewer and performer, small imperfections in the makeup will often pass unnoticed. A certain roughness of execution is even desirable for characters whose faces should show the effects of wind and weather, the blotchiness of disease or drink. There are other situations, however, in which such delicacy is called for that the audience remains in doubt whether any cosmetics at all have been employed. Most of the applications discussed in this chapter are of this nature.

Photographs, Television, and Film

In film, the camera's eye is the spectator's and can approach to within inches of the actor's face. At that short distance, it must be fooled into accepting paint and powder as flesh. Like Viola in *Twelfth Night*, the camera is a tough critic:

OLIVIA: (unveiling her face) Is't not well done?
VIOLA: Excellently well done, if God did all.

And like Olivia, the performer's job is to persuade the camera that "'Tis in grain, sir, 'twill endure wind and weather." Viola's reply holds the key to making up for photography: "'Tis beauty truly blent, whose red and white / Nature's own sweet and cunning hand laid on" (1.5).

Perfect blending is a necessity. Paint must be so cunningly laid on that colors and shapes merge seamlessly. Massive alterations can be attempted with carefully smoothed derma wax, but generally a prosthesis will be required. By and large, the actor must be content with small changes, modest thinnings and thickenings, and trust to hairstyle and costume to do the rest.

Notwithstanding, it is amazing what the actor can get away with by dint of a steady hand and wise design. The writer persuaded a television makeup artist to let her do her own makeup for Grandma in *The American Dream*, a role she had been playing for several months off Broadway. Then in the blush of youth, she was able to pass as that feisty ancient using exactly the same makeup as for the stage version, only more restrained in color and meticulously blended.

If possible, consult with the director of photography about what type of film and lighting will be used. Cosmetics are put out in color ranges expressly for film. Softer, muted shades generally work best. Primary colors—harsh reds, greens, and blues—are better avoided unless there has been special provision for them in the lighting.

Opera

At the opposite end of the spectrum is makeup for opera. In the enormous theatres that are standard for opera and musicals, subtle makeup would be lost on at least three-quarters of the house. Some adjustment will be necessary. According to Dan Duro, technical production director for the Santa Fe Opera, the main difference between opera and straight drama is scale. "You are less likely to get into the finer nuances with many things—character, scenery, costuming. Everything is in broader strokes for opera. The other difference, of course, is that actors begin with acting, but singers begin with the music. A singer's task is much more arduous: acting, moving, and singing at the same time." While conceding that opera singers are not, as a rule, required to refine their presentation of character as much as actors, Duro looks forward to a change in this pattern, citing his own company as a pioneer in this respect. "Frequent rehearsals over a long period have helped us to avoid the 'brown and serve' syndrome that typifies many opera productions. We encourage our singers to be more up-to-date and interesting as actors. Singers need to be more competitive with actors, and to develop the ability to present themselves in a character."

His company values performer expertise in matters of makeup. "All apprentices and intermediate-level singers and many of the principals at the Santa Fe Opera do their own makeups, unless there is a special problem, and have their own makeup kits." He notes: "Self-reliance in general leads to a better performance."

Character dictates makeup in opera as in all drama, but the makeup must carry an equivalent of several city blocks and is therefore bolder and more masklike than for smaller stages. Modeling is nevertheless essential if the character's humanity is to be preserved. As operatic performance is refined to reflect the inner drama, so too will operatic makeup inevitably move away from its present emphasis on mascara and false eyelashes toward faces that reveal the person who gives rise to the song (fig. 25).

Readings, Recitals, and Lectures

For these situations, characterization is not usually required; the performer is appearing as himself, and the audience assumes he is as he appears. This is not inevitably the case; lectures and readings provide legitimate occasions for using corrective makeup (see chapter 14). Women, particularly, can take advantage of the lecture platform to improve on nature. Remember, however, that the result may have to pass close inspection afterward at the cocktail party or faculty gathering that frequently follows these events.

Auditions: The Art of Subliminal Salesmanship

Tootsie remains the definitive example of a makeup that got the part. It is not usually necessary to go to the extreme of transvestism in order to convince a producer that you deserve the role. Nevertheless, a great deal of thought prior to appearing before anyone who has anything to do with casting is advisable.

No job requires more imagination than that of casting head. Before there is scenery, lighting, or costume, casting people must review scores, even hundreds, of aspirants in mufti and try to determine what each will

Fig. 25. Elaine Bonazzi as Herodias in the opera *Salome* by Richard Strauss. Photograph by Ken Howard, courtesy the Santa Fe Opera.

look like from the audience on opening night. Some are adept at this pre-visualization, but others, alas, have the imagination of cabbages and must be shown the finished product. All are vulnerable to subtle and not-so-subtle hints that can help to trigger a yes response. To ignore the question of physical impact at an audition and go "neutral" is to invite rejection out of hand. Remember, your neutral may be another person's far out. The writer recalls watching an actress audition for the part of Juliet wearing spike heels, a pompadour, false eyelashes, heavy mascara, and burgundy wet-look lipstick. The actress was thunderstruck when the director failed to see her as a fourteen-year-old.

Many circumstances will affect your decision about how much to look the part when auditioning. Obviously, it is more difficult to pull the wool over the eyes of those who know you well. If you have auditioned or worked for your examiner previously or expect to do so in the near future, you will think twice about establishing in his or her mind an indelible image of a specific "you." However, when it is a one-shot event, or if you are desperate for one reason or another to gain a particular role, it is worth going all out to make the desired impression. Skirts can be lengthened or shortened, necklines raised or lowered, ties added, removed, or loosened, hair restyled or a wig worn. Color sends a powerful message: clothing colors can be heightened or toned down.

Makeup can be left off entirely or used very subtly to suggest character. For example, the simple expedient of angling the eyebrows very slightly down on the inside corners can convey an air of menace, a useful touch if you are the kind who is constantly being typecast as Mr. Nice Guy or Ms. Goody Two-Shoes. Clothing, jewelry, and shoes can add to the effect you are cultivating. A dirndl skirt or a shawl for a peasant woman, a loud tie for the Gentleman Caller, a good sports jacket for Henry Higgins, send the proper message without shouting. Audition make-up and clothing works like perfume—a hint is all you need.

Just for the Fun of It

People who combine a keen sense of style with unabashed self-confidence frequently are able to appear in clothes most of us would wear only in our dreams. Their faces and attire proclaim to the world, "This is what I feel myself to be at the moment, and it feels good!" Sting's chains, Streisand's white sable collars, Labelle's roller-coaster hairdo, Liberace's sequins, Elton John's eyeglasses, Louise Nevelson's coal black eye sockets and tight bandana bespeak a daring that makes lesser spirits blanch.

There is no reason, however, why ordinary men and women cannot indulge their fantasies to at least some degree by the way they dress or fix their hair. Sometimes we feel funky, sometimes svelte. With a solid knowledge of period styles and a little imagination, it is possible to "outfit" a mood, reinforcing it to produce a feeling of personal power and well-being. The clothing and cosmetics industries already encourage us to take this path, urging us to buy this or that item in order to feel stronger, sexier, more in control, or just plain "with it." Men don leather jackets, boots, and scarves to feel like army pilots. Women in purple lipstick and tight jeans reincarnate Madonna by the thousands. The choice remains with each individual to run with the pack or strike out, modestly but with a certain dash, to be the "you" that suits your fancy. Appendixes B–G, on period styles, and both chapter 12 and chapter 14 will provide guidance. Just remember, your audience is not in the last row of the orchestra but standing beside you at the next traffic light.

Study Projects

1. Pick a character you would enjoy playing and imagine that a production of the play in which that character appears has been announced. Dress and make up for your audition. Do a typical speech from the play and see if your classmates agree that your clothes, accessories, and makeup give you a casting advantage.

2. Bring an instant camera to class and take snapshots of the audition makeups. Which ones are subtle enough to photograph as "no makeup" or acceptable street makeup?

Part II

Execution: An Actor's Manual on Makeup

Introduction

The Purpose and Paraphernalia of Makeup

Purpose

1. Makeup restores three dimensions and color to the face, flattened and bleached by strong light and distance.

2. Makeup creates for the audience a visual image of the character and for the performer the sense of a physical and mental "other."

3. Makeup gives the performer the psychological protection of disguise.

Equipment

The Makeup Box

Whether in the heart of New York City or the wilds of Saskatchewan, an actor's makeup kit is truly a home away from home. It functions as drugstore, five-and-dime, sewing basket, vanity, first aid station, and petty cashbox. It provides instant assistance when time is short and there is no access to stores.

Tackleboxes or small overnight cases with a variety of compartments that display their contents easily are widely used, but you will probably want to customize yours to fit your personal requirements. Perhaps yours will have a section set aside for contact lens paraphernalia, a padded drawer for costume jewelry, or a cache of coins for precurtain telephoning. Your dressing room has no running water? No matter, the tiny squeeze bottle stowed away in the bottom contains enough for one or two applications of pancake. If you are nearsighted and must contort your body like a double-jointed acrobat in order to see your face in the mirror, you will have contrived a portable mirror that clamps cleverly to the lid at precisely the right angle to accommodate your myopia (fig. 26).

It need not be as elaborate as the "Traveling Equipage" owned by Ferdinand VI of Spain, a case containing sixty-eight assorted utensils, a gold earpick, and a concealed music box—but nothing should be lacking to confront emergency. Be sure and keep the kit light by leaving at home items you don't need for the job at hand. Mammoth jars of powder and cleansing cream should be taken only if you are performing in the same place for many weeks. You will appreciate featherweight when you are

Fig. 26. A customized makeup kit adapted to the needs of a nearsighted performer.

trying to wrestle suitcase, garment bag, and makeup box into a crowded bus or taxi. A lock will forestall dumping the contents in the middle of Times Square as well as provide overnight security at the theatre.

Essential Tools

With slight adjustments, the following will supply the needs of both men and women:

- Cake makeup
- Grease (pots, tubes, sticks) for base
- Lining colors (smaller jars, tins, or sticks)
- Two flat square-tip one-fourth-inch brushes (cheaper in an art supply)*
- Eyebrow pencils: black and brown
- Single-edge razor blade
- Mascara; eye shadow; eyelash adhesive; lashes
- Rouge: dry and moist
- Powder (white talcum or translucent)
- Flat powder puffs, sponges (natural), cotton swabs
- Small emergency package of facial tissues
- Small scissors
- Wooden sculptor's tool or orange stick
- Small combination comb and brush
- Bobby pins, hairpins, hatpins, hairnet
- Small sewing kit
- Crepe wool (assorted colors)
- Gauze squares or roll
- Spirit gum, spirit gum remover
- Derma wax (mortician's putty)
- Acetone (small bottle, tightly capped)
- Cleansing cream or lotion (small amount)
- Bandaids, antiseptic, aspirin
- Aluminum watercolor box for mixing (two by seven inches)
- Small strip of watercolor paints for repairs
- Small hotel soap; compressed washcloth

*Cut the wooden stems to no more than five inches in length to avoid inadvertently putting an eye out as you lean into your makeup mirror.

Good to have: Makeup bib or gown; heating coil for making hot water; collapsible cup; coins, postage stamps; lots of safety pins in assorted sizes; small pencil and pad; tiny gooseneck lamp, small flashlight.

Special items needed for a particular role. Depending on the role, things like artificial blood, hair whitener, latex, tooth wax, body makeup, glycerine for sweat, etc.

Add your own. (toothbrush? contact lenses? nail clipper?)

_____

_____

_____

The Workplace

Unless you have the star dressing room, it is up to you to carve out a space in which you can work in relative peace and quiet. Your immediate surroundings are as important an aid to the creation of the image as are the paints and brushes. Arrange the area assigned to you for the greatest convenience, checking for:

· Lights (a colored-gel system is ideal but rare)*
· Three-way mirror (the audience sees the back of your head and so must you)
· Shelves, drawers, hangers, hooks, costume rack
· Wastebasket
· Sink, towels, soap, toilet facilities

*Important note: Shield the bulbs that surround the makeup mirror or turn them off and get a flexible lamp. Hang this so that the light comes from above and casts an even, nonglaring illumination that permits you to see what you are doing without being blinded. The traditional halo of naked bulbs is a Hollywood fantasy. Dazzling light is good for testing the finished makeup and for nothing else.

You are now ready to begin applying makeup, after a preliminary examination of your face.

8

Know What's There

The Bare Bones

Sit at a mirror and give your face the kind of searching examination that Richard II gives his in the deposition scene. Learn what parts of it are overly long, short, round, flat. Those blessed with cheekbones will have no difficulty finding them. Others will need to probe with their fingers for the hollows and ridges that exist beneath the flesh. Memorize the shade of your hair and skin; notice whether your eyebrows grow in a straight line or arch high above the eye. Is the eye cradled in its socket by well-formed upper and lower lids or does a flap of skin hang over the top of it, partially obscuring the eyeball? Is there a firm chin? Is there any chin at all? Do not despair. There are ways of getting one.

The Bones Fleshed Over

Survey the whole field. Out of sight is often out of mind. Beginners can always be detected by their attitude in front of the mirror. Most plant themselves foursquare to the glass as if daring it to reflect any but the most complimentary view. Head high, eyelids at half mast they view a very limited terrain rather uncritically. In this head-on confrontation, double chins are smoothed, wrinkles disappear, and cheekbones rise miraculously where none existed. Wing ears are becomingly foreshortened and aquiline noses turn pug. Thus locked in position, they proceed to apply paint to features that are not where the actor thinks they are, with grotesque results. An honest examination now, head on, not head up, will avoid grief later on (figs. 27 and 28).

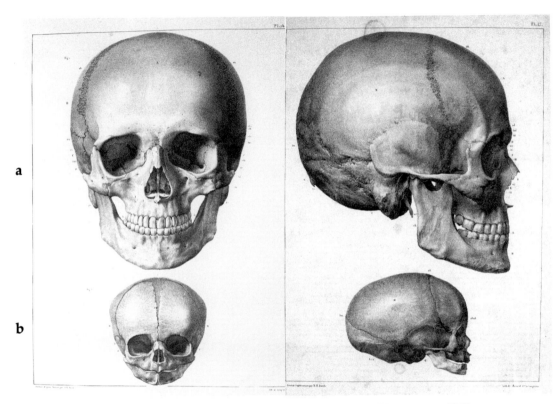

a

b

Fig. 27. Bones of the skull, front and side: adult *(a)*, child *(b)*. From an 1833 anatomy book, courtesy Richard Fitch, Americana.

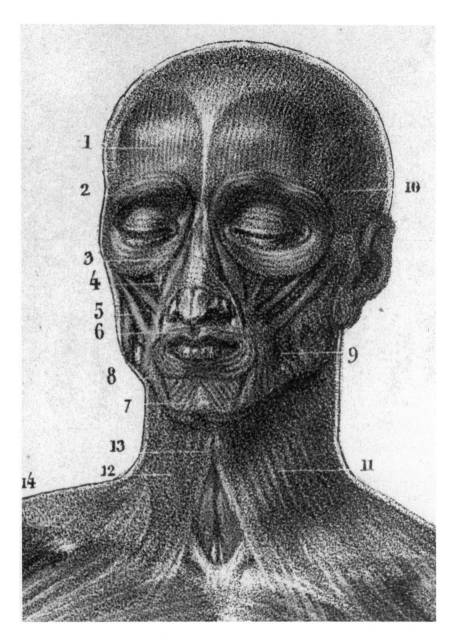

Fig. 28. Facial muscles. Courtesy Richard Fitch, Americana.

Facial Planes

Artists have viewed the face in many ways. In fact, whole movements in art have started with new and startling depictions of the human countenance (fig. 29). Early in the twentieth century, cubists and futurists broke up the face into planes and volumes (the kind of thing that French cartoonists had done even earlier in portraying a head of Louis Napoleon entirely composed of vegetables). In order to grasp the basic problem makeup poses, it is necessary to see the face as they saw it—a field in which two events constantly recur (fig. 30):

1. Two flat planes meet sharply at an angle to each other.
2. A curved surface, convex or concave, rises gradually from the surrounding area or sinks gently into it.

Since we have said that strong light and distance tend to flatten, shrink, and bleach color from the face, the first challenge of stage makeup is clear: to restore three dimensionality and normal size to the features. Makeup does this by taking advantage of the painter's ability to create optical illusions. Simply put, makeup, skillfully applied, can force the audience to accept an illusion as truth.

Fig. 29. Cubist image.

Fig. 30. Forms found in the human face.

9

Basic Principles and Practice Exercises

Basic Principles

Paint creates illusion by:

1. Using dark and light color to create or restore depth or prominences. Principle: Light colors come forward, dark colors recede.

2. Emphasizing hard and soft edges to replicate sudden or gradual changes in the facial planes.

3. Overriding the actual forms of a face to create a different form than exists naturally. Principle: The eye of the spectator, following the path of least resistance, will look where the paint directs it to look and perceive the altered feature as real.

Mixing Your Main Colors

The three main colors you will need to start with are:
- A base color
- A highlight color that is a mixture of white and base
- A shadow color that is a mixture of brown and base

Choose for your base coat, which will represent your general skin tone, a color two to three shades darker than your skin (remember the bleaching effect of strong light). Now you will need a smaller amount of pure white and pure brown (these are called lining colors or creme liners in the catalogs). You will never use *pure* brown or *pure* white to model your features unless you are making up for Fantasy. What you are after is the natural look of flesh. Therefore your highlight and shadow colors need to be alloys of your base. By mixing each with a little base, you have put your three basic colors in the same "family" and guaranteed a homogeneous look to the face. Select a warm, reddish brown to begin your shadow mixture. It will give a more natural color than a brown that contains green or blue; these, when mixed with base, tend to go muddy. For some makeups, you will eventually want more than one shadow color, for example a bluish color for the deepest recesses of the eye socket if the character is ill or emaciated.

Other Materials Needed

Palette

A child's small tin paintbox with the watercolor strip removed makes an excellent palette and has the added advantage of a lid that will keep the dust off unused paint overnight. Life will be infinitely easier if you keep one brush for shadow and one for highlight between the fingers of your nonworking hand and NEVER dip one into the other's color.

Miscellaneous

You will also find the following useful: two flat, square-tipped one-fourth-inch brushes with the handles trimmed to five inches or less in length, black or brown eyebrow pencil, powder, puff, tissue, cleansing cream.

Face Preparation

Secure any loose hair, protect shoulders and lap with suitable covering. Prepare for making up by washing hands and face with soap and water (easier said than done if you find yourself, as we once did, in a National Park barracks from which the actors had to sortie in midwinter to a well-pump in the in the middle of a pasture. In such a case, use cleansing cream or astringent.) Cleanliness is essential, for it is usually not the makeup that causes your skin to break out but the rubbing in of dirt. Use light, quick strokes in applying makeup and avoid dragging on the skin. Grease and powder are best spread by patting, not rubbing.

Applying the Base

Remove any excess cleansing cream if you have used it. Modern theatrical cosmetics do not generally need a cold cream underlayment. Lay down a thin, dry coat of base color, dotting it on rather sparingly and moving it well into the creases around nostrils and under the eyes. For performance, extend it as far down the neck and up into the hairline as necessary for complete coverage (see chapter 16). Pat off the excess with tissue—base should be matte and dry, not gooey.

In the exercises that follow, shadows and highlights are applied over the base. This is the most usual method, but it is also possible to complete the modeling without a base and then mitigate the harsh effect this gives by sponging cake makeup over the greasepaint. This method is useful for quick changes when, by carefully rinsing off the top layer, another character or the same one at a different age is revealed.

If, when using grease, you find the base hard to spread, dip your fingers in cold water and the grease will go on more smoothly.

Practice Exercises

In the following six exercises it should be clear that you will be dealing with your face as it is, NOT attempting to create a person of a different nationality or a character with features other than your own. Color selection and mixing will be discussed later. For now, all you will need are the three basic colors mentioned above. Carefully study the exercises and the notes that accompany them, as all future work will be based upon them.

l. Hard Edges: The Nose

Identify a place on the face where two flat planes meet at an angle. In other words, where the planes of the face go suddenly from dark to light. Chances are you have homed in on the front and sides of the nose. Proceed as shown in figures 31–34.

1 (fig. 31). Lay down shadow color (brown mixed with base until three shades darker than base color) along each side of the center ridge.

2 (fig. 32). Brush shadow carefully away from ridge and feather onto cheek. Note how much easier it is to do this with a square brush than with a pointed one.

3 (fig. 33). Lay a line of highlight color (white mixed with a little base) down the center of the nose from bridge to tip. Spread this by patting. Put a dot of highlight color on each nostril and pat the edges until they disappear.

4 (fig. 34). Pat hard edge with the finger to soften just a bit: flesh, after all, is not cardboard.

Note l: NEVER allow highlight to cross over a hard edge. Always blend AWAY from a hard edge. When diffusing a round or oval highlight, leave a narrow no-man's-land of base between the fade-out of the highlight and the beginning of a shadowed area.

Note 2: SQUINT at each feature as you complete it. Notice how the use of highlight and shadow gives the feature three dimensions, even from across the room or in strong light.

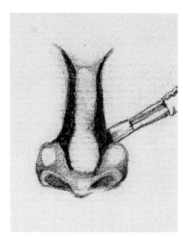

Figure 31

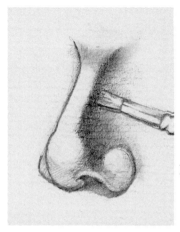

Figure 32

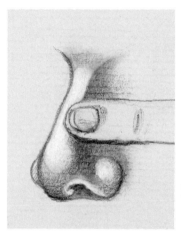

Figure 33

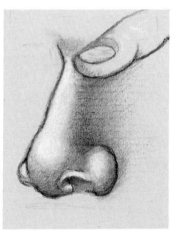

Figure 34

2. *Soft Edges: The Cheek*

Identify a place where a rounded surface rises smoothly and gradually from the surrounding area or sinks into it. That is, where the light change is a gradual one. The cheek is a good one to start with. Proceed as shown in figures 35–38.

1 (fig. 35). Feel for the hollow under your cheekbone. Put a dot of shadow color about the size of a nickel in the deepest part of the hollow and pat it out with a finger until it becomes a triangle. Leave most of the color in the deepest part of the hollow.

2 (fig. 36). Feather out at the edges so that the shadow fades to nothing in all directions, but be sure to keep the triangular shape. (This is harder to do than it seems.)

3 (fig. 37). Lay down a line of highlight color along the cheekbone ridge. Feather by patting top and bottom, leaving the brightest area on the crest of the ridge.

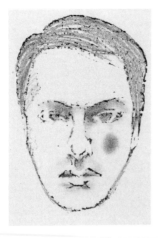

Figure 35

Figure 36

4 (fig. 38). Pat out any blotchiness. Make sure that a no-man's-land of base stays visible between the shadow area and the beginning of the highlight.

Figure 37

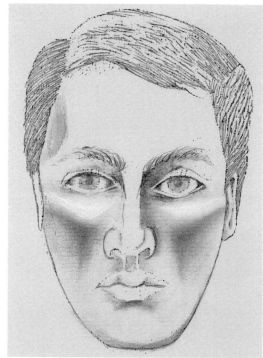

Figure 38

Note 3: It is very important to remember that every shadow has its corresponding highlight. No feature is complete until both have been painted in. (The only exception to this is a quick change, when a dab of highlight to bring the feature up is all you have time for.)

Note 4: Prudence dictates that you finish one feature at a time to avoid going onstage with a nostril missing.

Note 5: Remember to use separate brushes for highlight and shadow and to keep the colors separate and clean on your palm and palette.

3. Hard and Soft Edges: The Eye

All features display either hard or soft edges or a combination of the two. Complex features like the eyes and mouth have both hard edges (eye socket, upper lip) and soft (brow ridge, middle of lips). Proceed as shown in figures 39–44.

1 (fig. 39). Apply shadowing color in a somewhat light value uniformly to the whole upper eyelid and socket (an area that is naturally in shadow). Close the eye slightly and run a line of much darker shadow around the eyeball, pressing the brush firmly along the socket edge.

2 (fig. 40). Now blend UP from the edge of the socket, letting the shadow fade out before it gets to the eyebrow. Notice that the shape of this shadow is broader at the outer edge and narrower at the inner corner of the eye.

3 (fig. 41). Lay an oval highlight on the prominent fleshy area under the outer edge of the eyebrow. Feather the circumference out, leaving the center bright. Women: now dust on colored eye shadow if desired. POWDER the whole lid area so it doesn't smear, before continuing.

4 (fig. 42). Lightly shadow the shelf under the eye. (Feel for it as it cups the lower part of the eyeball.) POWDER under the eye to prevent smearing, before continuing.

5 (fig. 43). Apply eyeliner to edge of upper lid, just above lashes. Whether you use pencil or liquid for this, make sure to soften the line with a brush or your finger. (See Note 6.)

6 (fig. 44). Pencil in each hair of the eyebrow individually, bearing down heavier at the root and easing up on the stroke at the ends of the hairs. Pencil the eyebrows AFTER powdering so that the hairs aren't greasy. Use a sharp pencil, and make light strokes in the direction the hairs grow. Be sure to leave space between the strokes. Too solid eyebrows look pasted on. Add false eyelashes and mascara if desired. The lower lashes should be treated lightly unless the stage is very large.

Note 6: Both men and women will use eyeliner or dark shadow color to define the eye, but it should be softened and blended so it doesn't look like a painted line, unless you are striving for that effect.

Figure 39

Figure 40

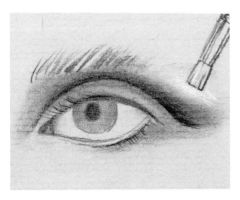

Figure 41

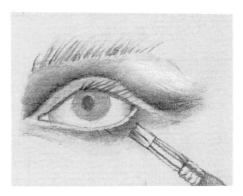

Figure 42

Figure 43

Figure 44

4. Hard and Soft Edges: The Mouth and Chin

Proceed as shown in figures 45–50.

1 (fig. 45). As in the eye exercise, apply an underlayment of light shadow to both lips after wiping off most of the base there.

2 (fig. 46). Apply a line of shadow down the center and sides of the depression in the center of the upper lip. Pat to diffuse the center shadow and blend AWAY from the hard edges of the side shadows. This is the shape a mustache takes, but it will not look like one if lightly done. It will merely give a natural form to the upper lip.

3 (fig. 47). Add highlight along the two ridges under the nose and along the entire edge of the upper lip. Soften the highlights slightly.

4 (fig. 48). Smear some medium dark shadow on the underside of the upper lip. This may be tinted with maroon, but men will want little color here. Use a finger rather than a brush for a more natural look. Model the "bumps" in the lips with shadow and highlight. A bump in the middle of the upper lip is common. Very full lips may have smaller puffs to each side. Generally, one or two highlights on the lower lip are enough.

5 (fig. 49). Outline the edge of the lower lip with medium shadow. Blend DOWNWARD, shaping around the bump of the chin, as indicated.

6 (fig. 50). Finish by highlighting the extreme edge of the lower lip, as you did the upper, dotting the ball of the chin with a highlight blended outward from the center. (Cleft chins have two highlights.) It's best to powder the lips as you finish them for the same reason as in exercise 3.

Note 7: Ladies, the question of lipstick must be faced. If you want the look of lipstick, use lipstick, but if you wish to have a mouth, you must model it as the men do. A compromise is to model in three values of the same shade of red—light, dark, and the color you want your lips to read (see chapter 10).

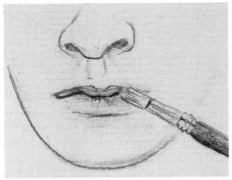

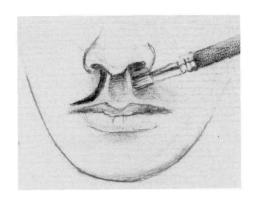

Figure 45   Figure 46

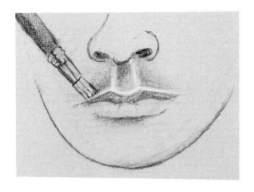

Figure 47   Figure 48

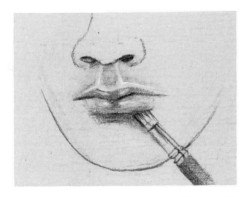

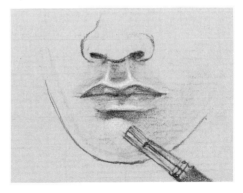

Figure 49   Figure 50

5. Hard and Soft Edges: The Forehead

Proceed as shown in figures 51–53.

1 (fig. 51). Press a finger into your temple and feel for the semicircular depression there, about the size of a fifty-cent piece. Lay a line of shadow following the bone ridge. Blend AWAY from the ridge toward the hairline. Highlight the ridge, blending AWAY from the shadow's hard edge toward the center of the face.

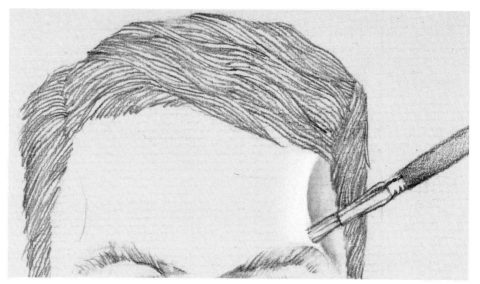

Figure 51

2 (fig. 52). Feel the round, half-a-grapefruit shape of the forehead. Is it a single dome or more like two smaller domes side by side? Outline the bottom of the shape with shadow, blending UP and toward the center of the forehead.

3 (fig. 53). Dot a highlight where the forehead is most prominent (some foreheads, like some chins, will have two bumps, as mentioned.) Blend the edge out in all directions. Add a broad swath of highlight along the brow ridge. Blend UP, being careful not to cross the hard edge of the forehead shadow.

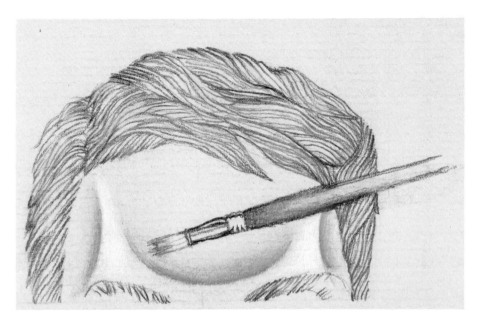

Figure 52

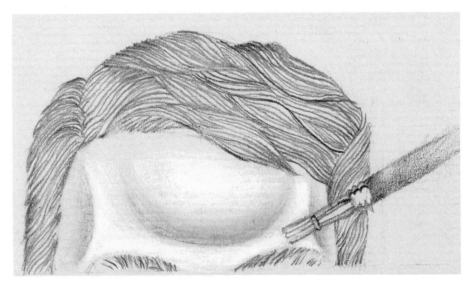

Figure 53

6. Wrinkles, Folds, and Bags

Life may begin at forty, but so do wrinkles. In preparation for our discussion of age (chapter 13) let us investigate three of the inevitable concomitants of the aging process: wrinkles, folds, and bags. Observe an older person's face. Remember that all features display either hard or soft edges or a combination of both. Observe that none display "lines." Even the tiniest wrinkle or crowsfoot forms a half cylinder beginning in shadow and gradually getting lighter as more light hits the surface from above and in front, as it does in nature and on the stage. The light is strongest at the feature's highest point, and that is where the highlight is brightest.

Bags and folds under the eyes and around the cheeks, mouth, and chin are treated the same as wrinkles, that is, with one hard edge and a highlight on the most prominent part. Proceed as shown in figures 54–57.

1 (fig. 54). Wrinkle your forehead and observe where it creases naturally. Now RELAX it and lay a line of shadow under the first wrinkle. Interrupt the shadow in one or two places for a more natural look. Blend up from the hard edge. Notice what a short space you have to do this. Before adding the highlight, do the next higher shadow. This will give you the boundary that your highlight must not cross.

2 (fig. 55). Now lay in the highlight for the first wrinkle and carefully soften it with a brush without crossing the shadow above or obliterating the tiny no-man's-land of base below it. Do several more wrinkles.

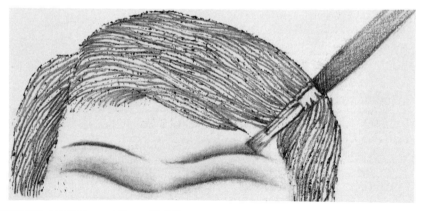

Figure 54

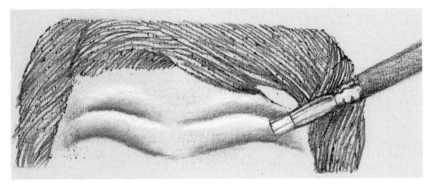

Figure 55

3 (fig. 56). Crow's feet are handled the same as forehead wrinkles. DO NOT LET THEM RADIATE FROM ONE POINT. The concentration of paint will form a blob. Start each at least one-eighth inch from the next one, to reproduce the way they actually appear to the eye.

Figure 56

Note 8: For large theatres or a particularly "snappy" look, a thin accent highlight can be laid down next to a hard edge of shadow. Alternatively, the whole highlight can be moved up from the center of the wrinkle, to start right under the shadow of the next higher wrinkle. The lowest wrinkle in figure 55 has been done this way.

4 (fig. 57). Coil a line of shadow around the nostril and down in a curve around the upper jawline and across under the cheek. Blend AWAY from the nose. Leaving an area of base, lay in the highlight, following the same shape. Soften by patting. Undereye bags can be done the same way.

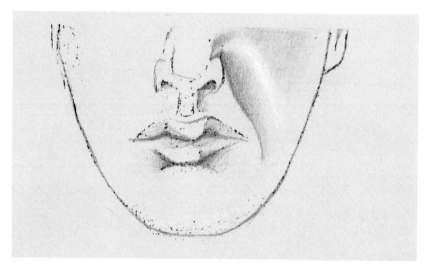

Figure 57

Finishing Touches

You have already powdered eyes and mouth, features that, because of their extreme mobility, will tend to smear. Now powder the whole face thoroughly, not rubbing, but pressing the powder into all the crevices. Use a cotton swab for small or hard to reach areas. A wide range of powder colors is available, but if you think about it, it is hardly worthwhile selecting the perfect base, highlight, and shadow colors for the role only to send them into oblivion under a veil of pink or amber powder. Translucent or white talcum powder disappears into base and will not change the underlying colors. Remember to pencil the eyebrows and apply mascara AFTER powdering.

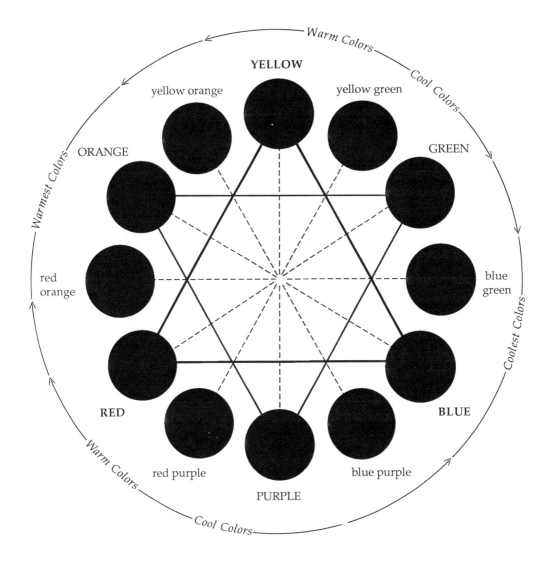

Fig. 58. Color wheel showing primary colors (dark triangle) and complementaries (dotted lines). Remember this refers to pigment and fabric colors, not to light. The wheel also indicates the gradations from warm to cool.

10

Color Selection and Mixing

Note: Demonstrations and examples throughout this book assume the use of greasepaint because mixing and blending are easier to do in that medium. Almost all of the same effects can be gotten with pancake or, when some skill has been developed, with a mixture of pancake and grease.

Color Choices

A major manufacturer of makeup products lists no less than fifty-two different shades of color for the face. Given this abundance of riches, it is easy to overlook the fact that all of these colors were derived from the three primaries, red, yellow, and blue, and that the entire spectrum consists of only three additional hues: orange, green, and purple. Throw in black, brown, white, and gray for good measure, and the actor has the capability of reproducing from these ten any of the fifty-two wanted. As the advertisers say, Why pay for what you don't need? A good base color or two is worth stockpiling. Otherwise, much of what you use can be mixed as needed from primaries. These come in smaller amounts called lining colors. There may be a slight loss of intensity when mixing colors, but it will not usually be enough to matter unless you are doing a highly decorative mask makeup. A good starter set of colors could include two or three shades of base and eight or nine lining colors: bright red, maroon, yellow, blue, green, black, white, and a warm brown.

Principles of Mixing Colored Pigments

The principles of mixing pigment colors are simple. Refer to the color wheel (fig. 58) as you read through them.

1. Mixing any two primaries will give an intermediate color that harmonizes with both primaries. Doing this (mixing red with yellow, yellow with blue, blue with red) adds three colors to the wheel, making a total of six colors.

2. The color directly opposite any color on the wheel is its complement. Mixing complements (e.g., red and green) produces a muddy gray or a brownish black.

3. Colors that have white in them or traces of another color too small to see may go muddy or pasty when mixed.

4. HUE is the name of the pure color, i.e., red, blue, green. INTENSITY indicates the degree of graying achieved by adding the complement to the color. The more intense, the purer the color because less of the complement has been added. VALUE refers to how light or dark color a color is, i.e., how close it is to white or black.

For a discussion of the effects of colored light on makeup colors, see chapter 21.

Study Projects

1. Mix from red, yellow, and blue (greasepaint or water colors) the three other spectrum colors: orange, green, and purple.

2. Gray each of the above colors, using its complement (opposite it, on the color wheel (fig. 58).

3. Using ONLY the three primaries and white, brown, and black, duplicate five colors taken at random from color swatches or a color illustration from a magazine.

11

Fine Blending and Stippling

A Tip from Leonardo and Seurat

In the previous exercises, you have practiced blending both with brush and finger. If you have discovered that you are all thumbs, do not be disheartened. It gets easier with practice. Actually, in a large theatre or for rough, weatherbeaten characters you may wish to leave the surface somewhat rude, textured, or blotchy. This effect can be achieved by stippling—dabbing the face lightly with a sponge laden with a color different from the base. Usually, two or more colors are used as in spattering scenery or in a painting by Seurat, and the blending is done by the audience's eye. Stippling can be put on after the regular makeup has been applied as a finishing layer. It is also used to tone down a makeup that is too strong.

For intimate playing spaces and for television and films, however, the more refined the blending, the greater the illusion of reality. The writer has been mistaken for others at a distance of three feet by dint of extremely subtle blending and color choice. Visit a museum and study Flemish and Italian painting of the Renaissance for examples of near-photographic realism achieved by using the same principles of blending that you are working from. Continue to develop your skill in this area. A good makeup is created by a daring leap of the imagination, but it must be executed by a hand that could defuse a bomb.

Study Projects

1. Visit a museum or study a good reproduction of a fifteenth-century Flemish portrait by Van der Weyden, Jan van Eyck, or Hans Memling. Also useful are the Florentine painters, particularly Leonardo da Vinci (1452–1519). Choose one feature from the painting you select and reproduce it on your own face as accurately as you can. Work to make the blending even and extremely gradual. Start, of course, by laying down a base extending beyond the feature to the surrounding facial area.

2. Using two or three shades of pancake, stipple the area you have marked out above with a sponge, to achieve the weathered, roughened look of a Bruegel peasant.

12

Changing the Features

Using Paint

Aging, beautifying, or conveying character all require a knowledge of how to make changes in the facial features. The key to doing this is Basic Principle #3. To review:

Basic Principle #3

OPTICAL ILLUSION: The eye of the audience, following the path of least resistance, will look where the paint directs it to look and perceive the altered feature as real.

In result terms, this means that if you can paint in a bump or a hollow where none exists and make the real ones seem to disappear, the audience's eye will accept the painted area as the reality.

Rules for Changing the Features with Paint

Remembering that light colors appear to come forward, while dark ones recede:
1. Lighten what you want to fatten or raise.
2. Darken what you want to slim down or sink.
3. Extend or shorten by going inside or outside and beyond a feature's natural borders.
4. Make BIG changes that will carry.
5. Make use of as much of what is already there as possible.

Paint Projects

Note the changing features as shown in figures 59 and 60 and then proceed with the projects.

1. Lengthen and thin your nose by using highlight and shadow.

2. Change the shape of your mouth or eyes by going inside or outside of their natural boundaries. Do not just draw an outline, but model the feature, using the principle of hard and soft edges (chapter 9).

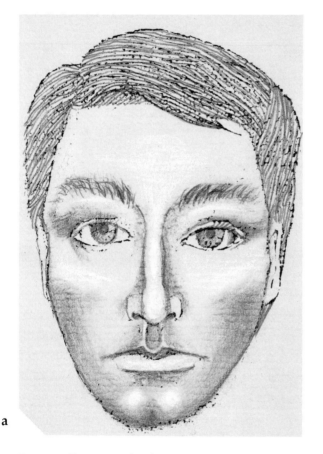

a

b

Fig. 59. Changing the features: Compare face (a) with original face (b). Man's face slimmed by shadowing the periphery; cheekbones defined; nose lengthened and thinned; eyebrows soaped out and reshaped; upper lip thinned by overriding edge; massive chin broken up by clefting.

Fig. 60. Changing the features: Compare face (a) with original face (b). Woman's eyes set farther apart by flattening bridge, keeping eyeshadow and eyeliner at outer extreme of eye and soaping out too-close inner edges of brows. Cheekbones less prominent and hard jawline softened by shadowing.

3. Slim down your face by shadowing around the periphery and sinking in the cheek hollows. Wipe off, and reapply base. Now fatten the face by lightening the periphery, modeling fat, fleshy cheeks with shadow and highlight, and raising any hollows.

4. Study male and female faces carefully. List or sketch the major differences. Make yourself up as a person of the opposite sex.

The Limits of Effective Change

Keep close to the natural contours of the features, going beyond them only when you must. Work the change in as a continuation of the natural form. Each face has limits beyond which it is impossible to make the illusion hold. A thin face can be fattened only so much, a firm neck will never be made by paint to swing in the wind like the wattles of a turkey.

If the change is too far-reaching to be accomplished with illusion, i.e., by paint and a little derma wax, you will need a prosthesis. To know this, have a friend critique your makeup from the audience. If your attempt at three chins registers as three painted circles, not flesh, at least one of those chins will need to be a prosthesis.

Using Prosthetic Devices

Putty and Derma Wax

The trick in changing the features is to make big changes that will carry, but to use as much of what is already there to accomplish this as you can. Thus, gaining a large nose does not necessarily require massive applications of nose putty: it may be that the bridge of the nose and the nostrils are big enough, and all you need is a bit of a bump at the tip. This can be modeled with putty or derma wax.

Technically prostheses, putty, and derma wax (also known as mortician's wax) are capable of performing the same miracle for the living as for the dead—the almost undetectable three-dimensional reconstruction of the features. Putty is initially harder than derma wax, but it is possible to combine the two substances if a firmer feature is needed. For many applications, derma wax alone will suffice. A very small amount of it goes a long way. Apply it to a squeaky clean surface. For greater security, spirit gum may be painted on the skin and a small fluff of cotton pressed into it; the derma wax is then forced down on the cotton, molded into the desired shape, and the excess feathered out to a disappearing edge. For this, an orange stick or a plastic or metal-capped eyebrow pencil is a good tool. The feature can be painted with latex if desired, before applying base and proceeding with shadow and highlight color. Powder, then test the result in the mirror from the side as well as front. A bold, well-integrated addition to a small area can radically alter the appearance of the whole face (fig. 61). Remove by running a nylon thread between the wax and the skin.

Other Materials

New materials and techniques have brought the prothesis a long way from the crude gauze constructions that were used in the past. Many pre-

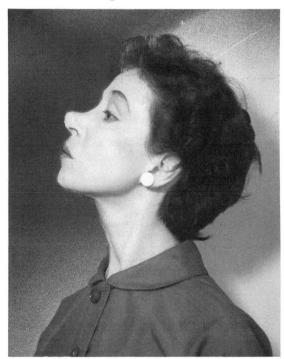

Fig. 61. Putty nose for the part of Mrs. Smith in *The Bald Soprano.*

formed structures are now obtainable that can be applied to the face even by amateurs. Others may be cut from latex Halloween and monster masks, of which there is a bewildering assortment. Casting the face (moulage) and customized jowls, chins, and cheeks made to measure are perhaps best left to the specialist. Prostheses do cut down mobility and often seem to be resorted to before other creative avenues are exhausted. Disdain for makeup's capabilities can stem from insufficient knowledge, failure of imagination, or lack of nerve. Try first what paint can do.

Warts, Moles, and Scars

Moles, warts, bruises, and scars present varying problems, and the first step in solving them is to attain a clear idea of the look you want to achieve. Is the blemish to be flat or raised? Raw and bleeding or fully healed? Is hair involved? A basic scar effect can be had by applying a dab or line of spirit gum and pinching the skin into a fold. When fully dry, the crease will remain in place and can be touched up with red and modeled with highlight and shadow. Alternatively, the edge can be built up with gauze, embedded with hairs, or roughened with cornmeal and then colored. Remember that whether you build up a wound or a mole three-dimensionally or paint it on, the same principles of hard and soft edges and contrast of light and shadow must be followed if the blemish is to look thoroughly realistic.

Latex and gelatin may also be used to make high relief eye pouches. Texturing of the pouch can be done by pressing in cornmeal, wheat germ, or, for a more delicate effect, the skin of a lemon before the construction is fully set.

Blind eyes and epicanthic folds (see chapter 17) can be constructed by painting latex over gauze or using plastic film laid over the eyelid. BE CAREFUL with adhesives or chemicals of any sort around the eyes. For coloring over latex, a special castor-oil-base greasepaint may be purchased.

Prosthetic Projects

1. Change the shape of your nose with derma wax, using just enough to give you the look you want (a broken nose? a Roman or eagle nose? a pug?). Cover carefully with base and apply highlight and shadow as you would to your own nose to make it read through light and across distance.

2. Create a fresh wound, either a cut or a sore, using the principles outlined in this section.

3. Re-create the same wound as a scar, the way it would look one or two years later.

4. Model a hairy wart that you might use as a troll in *Peer Gynt,* one of the witches in *Macbeth,* or a Fury in *The Eumenides.*

13

Age: Going Forward and Backward in Time

Old Age as a Continuum

Having briefed yourself on ways of altering the features, you are equipped to cope with the changes time brings, from infancy onward. Old age is thought of by the young—if they think of it at all—as something that happens suddenly to people who have grown careless. Youth harbors a suspicion that the elderly *could* stand up straight and keep their jaws together if they really wanted to. In actuality, old age is seldom a matter of choice and does not overtake one precipitously at thirty, forty-five, or seventy. It begins in the moment of full bloom (some would say at birth) and proceeds in a continuum of decay toward death and dissolution.

People do age differently; what the character has met with on the journey of life is more useful to know than the person's chronological age. This section does not deal with old age as if it were a mortgage payment that suddenly falls due. Rather it is concerned with how the human face changes from childhood on.

From Childhood Onward

Infant skulls are proportioned very differently from mature ones (see figure 27), and to a degree those differences are perpetuated into adolescence. Notice in figure 63 the flatness of the child's face, the low relief of the features and the prevalence of curves. Now come back to figure 62

Fig. 62. (a) The actress playing Rip Torn's mother is in her late thirties; photograph by Bert Andrews; (b) same actress in her twenties playing a child.

and see how angular and prominent the features are in adulthood and how differently space is aportioned in the face. Observe also how in age the flesh loses its ability to hold a shape and begins to sag under the pull of gravity.

Psychological and environmental factors reinforce heredity as the years advance. Call to mind the wide-eyed curiosity of the normal child, the way the very pores of the face appear to drink in new experience. Notice a child's delicate vulnerability and quick mood shifts. Then regard the iron-faced determination of the thirty-seven-year-old advertising executive as he struggles up the corporate ladder. Imagine that same man as an octagenarian on whom disease or mental illness has taken its toll.

Major Characteristics of Extreme Youth and Age

Just as there is no such thing as a "straight" makeup because all roles are character parts, there is no such thing as "old age" makeup, only people who have lived life easily or hard for a certain number of years. Still, it is possible to identify the major characteristics of extreme youth and age.

Removing Age (Figure 63)	Adding Age (Figure 64)
Short face	Longer face
Low relief	High relief
Hair glossy	Hair thin, gray or white
Domed forehead	Baldness
High eyebrow	Wrinkles
Fine hair	Bones protrude
Round eye	Shaggy eyebrows
Fat cheeks	Drooping folds
Low bridge	Bags, pouches
Button nostrils	Sunken hollows
Obtruded lips	Distortion
Small chin	Jowls
	"Prune" lips
	Bony chin
	Double chins
Rosy color	Usually pale
Smooth skin	Rougher skin

(See "6. Wrinkles, Folds, and Bags," chapter 9.)

Follow whatever wrinkles you possess naturally to avoid gaining two sets when you smile or crease your forehead. Eyebrows can be eliminated by smoothing them with a paste made of wet soap. This must be absolutely smooth; any lumps will show under the base. When the soap has dried, the hardened surface may be covered over with paint. Teeth may be aged or cracked by rubbing them with brown mustache wax, or they may be obliterated by covering them with black enamel or tooth wax.

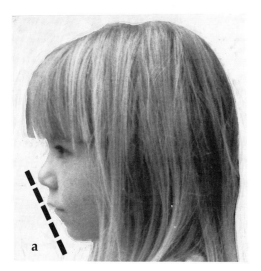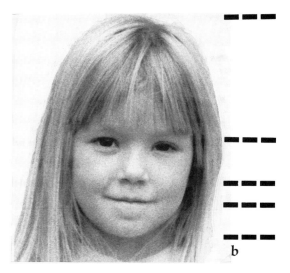

Fig. 63. The proportions of childhood: notice the small, rounded features, button nose (due to the absence of "bony" cartilage in the bridge). The underdeveloped jaw gives the profile its characteristic backward slant (a). In (b), notice the tiny space taken up by the eyes, nose, and mouth (within dotted lines) and the small chin, compared to the enormous expanse of forehead. (See also figure 27b: child's skull.)

Study Project

Pick two ages, one in childhood, the other between forty-five and seventy-five. Create an imaginary person and list the details of the person's character at each age chosen. Make up half of your face as the child and the other half as the same person older.

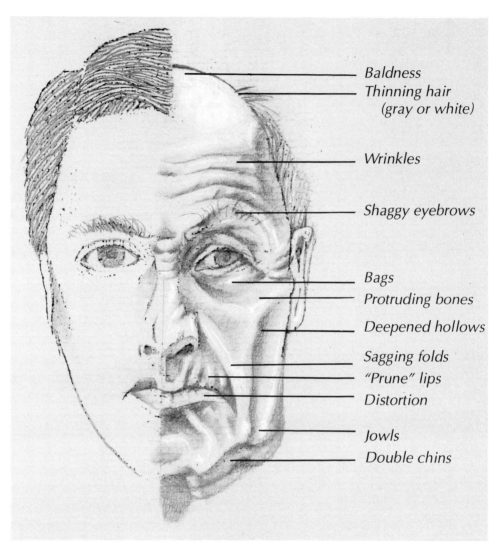

Baldness
Thinning hair
   (gray or white)

Wrinkles

Shaggy eyebrows

Bags
Protruding bones
Deepened hollows
Sagging folds
"Prune" lips
Distortion
Jowls
Double chins

Fig. 64. Aging the features: Identify the places where the bones become more prominent (temples, forehead, cheek) and areas where the flesh distorts, sags, or wrinkles (upper eyelid, under the eyes, nasolabial fold from nostril to mouth, "prune" lips, chin, jowels). Chins may be doubled or tripled and necks either fattened with horizontal folds of flesh or thinned and made scrawny, with prominent vertical cords on both sides of the Adam's apple.

14

Corrective Makeup

This subject should really not be listed as a separate chapter, for corrective makeup is what we have been dealing with all along, namely, the changing of the natural features to make them appear other than they are. What corrective makeup implies over and above the idea of change is an aesthetic judgment. It presupposes that the change will be an improvement over what was there before and that you will look "better."

What this constitutes is not simple to determine. It is easy to detail the steps required to achieve general states like fat, thin, old, or young. These are fairly straightforward goals, and models for them are easy to locate. It is harder to establish what is beautiful or plain, handsome or ugly. Fashions in facial beauty change with the changing seasons—a new hemline, a new "look." Beauty is very much in the eye of the beholder, and the beholder is a product of his or her time and place.

We in the Western world usually see beauty as a function of proportion and symmetry. Taking as our standard the classic images of ancient Greece, we tend to admire regularity of feature and to expect that the two sides of the face will match, although we know they seldom do. Our criterion is fraught with arbitrary rules and reversals. We disdain noses that are too big, but admire large, lustrous eyes. We look for full lips in women but not in men, from whom strong chins are demanded. We find fault with our own features, even though others find them pleasing, because they do not match this capricious ideal and set out to bring them into line by corrective makeup although we would be hard pressed to define what we mean by "correct."

In the end, corrective makeup is what makes you feel comely, so by all means smooth out that bump, arch that eyebrow, white out those bags until, like Cinderella's sisters, you are satisfied with what your mirror tells you. Just remember that variety is the spice of life and that Garbo had thin lips. (For a good example of a makeup that combines correction with characterization, see figure 65.)

Frequent Corrective Changes

Stage beautification differs from street makeup largely in achieving its ends by actually appearing to sculpt the features three-dimensionally, whereas street makeup relies for the most part on the application of flat color and line.

Adjustments Valid for Both Street and Stage Makeup

1. To shorten the nose, darken it under the tip with shadow color and dab the top of the tip with highlight.

2. To soften the jawline, shadow it lightly. To emphasize jawline or cheekbone, highlight them.

3. To narrow the face, shadow the periphery, bring the eyes closer together by extending the inner corners of eyes and eyebrows further toward the nose. Emphasize the length of the nose with a highlight down the center. Continue this under the tip if desired.

4. To widen the face, reverse the above by lightening the periphery and extending the eyes and brows at the outer edges.

Major Corrective Overhauls

Major overhauls will require more than paint. For those who, in the immortal words of Gypsy Rose Lee, have everything they had at twenty, only three inches lower, there are temporary facelifts made out of plastic adhesive tape or *mousseline de soie*. Tabs with strings attached may be pasted in front of each ear or on either side of a sagging neck just below the earlobe. The two strings are then tied together on the crown of the head, pulling the flesh taut. Personally, the writer believes the power of

Fig. 65. The actress *(insert)* showed her husband this picture of herself in costume and makeup. Said he: "How'd you manage that?" Theatrical photograph by Barbara Gordon.

adhesive tape and spirit gum can be sorely tried by hot lights, perspiration, and sudden movements. Faith may be better vested in the tensile strength of human hair. After all, acrobats hang by it, trusting their lives to its amazing ability to resist strain. If you have long hair, gather it into a topknot and pull it taut. Short hair may be gathered and bobby-pinned in several tight curls above the ears and on the crown of the head. Observe at what angle you need to pull the hair in order to lift eyes, cheeks, or chin. Flatten each knot or pincurl and secure it firmly with sufficient hairpins or bobby pins. Conceal the whole with a hat, scarf, wig, curls, or a fall.

Teeth that are yellowed or stained can be whitened with tooth enamel, which comes is a variety of shades. Black is useful for shortening what one actress calls "the family tombstones"—front teeth which are too long. (See also chapter 12.)

Study Projects

1. Using the principles in this chapter, make over one or more features of your face to conform to your idea of handsomeness or beauty. Use derma wax if necessary, but do the most you can with paint.

2. Pick a partner and "correct" the features of his or her face to meet a generally accepted standard of physical beauty. Reverse roles.

15

Hair

Performers enjoy much more flexibility in choosing how they will wear their hair onstage than they do in private life. Most of us settle for one or two styles that we believe best suit our faces, but in the theatre the possibilities are virtually unlimited because the actor creates a new body and face for every role.

Choosing a Hairstyle

Ordinarily, hair shape and color will evolve along with the character image. Choose the style that is best for your character. Do not be afraid that it will be unbecoming: remember that you will be making substantial changes in your features and can therefore experiment with wearing your hair in ways you never dared to try before.

Hair's dramatic possibilities can be multiplied by the addition of hair ornaments, flowers, feathers, and, of course, hairpieces of all kinds. Men have the further weaponry of mustaches, sideburns, and beards.

What Hair Can Do

Hair color and styling can do any or all of the following:

Change the proportions of the face. Hair can add inches of height, broaden or slim the face. Notice in figures 66 and 67 how hair can widen the head at temples or chin, bisect a too-high forehead, lengthen the head.

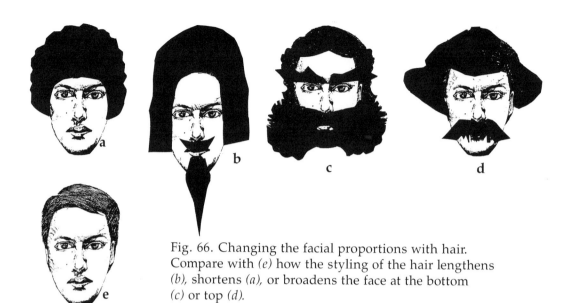

Fig. 66. Changing the facial proportions with hair. Compare with *(e)* how the styling of the hair lengthens *(b)*, shortens *(a)*, or broadens the face at the bottom *(c)* or top *(d)*.

Fig. 67. Changing the facial proportions with hair. Compare with *(c)* the emphasizing of a triangular face shape *(a)* and its conversion to a long oval by means of hairstyling *(b)*.

Set chronological age. Although long hair is usually associated with childhood and youth, notice how a cap of short hair says "child" in figure 62. (The actress is in her late twenties.) Upswept hair and elaborate coiffures, on the other hand, add years and even a hint of gray or white can convey instant senior citizenship.

Indicate period. Like airplanes, costume and hair are easily identified by period, just from a silhouette. If you are using hair to set period, study the unique features of each era and choose one of the most representative styles (fig. 68*a, b, c,* and see also appendixes B–G on period styles).

a   b   c

Fig. 68. Hair to set the period: (*a*) student in the part of a nineteenth-century girl rescued from drowning (Columbia University production). (*b*) Byzantine king, courtesy Four Winds Theatre. (*c*) Wig (made from an inexpensive street wig) for a documentary on Ancient Egypt, performed at the Metropolitan Museum of Art. Photographs by William McGonigle.

Convey character. The bedraggled Eliza Doolittle was turned into a duchess simply by keeping a watch on her tongue and restyling her hair. Clearly, how we fix our hair influences what kind of person we are judged to be. Our state of mental and physical health, taste, social circle, and other factors can be reflected in the pains we do or do not take with our hair (fig. 68*a*). An air of fussiness or abandon may be conveyed with a profusion of curls or frizz (fig. 69). Keeping the hair sleek and close to the head suggests sobriety or plainness. (See also chapter 4.)

Coloring, Graying, Streaking

Hair may be temporarily colored with a hair spray or with cake makeup, but the latter should be put on with a light hand or it will look like dried plaster. For quick changes, a single streak can also be made out of crepe hair and attached permanently to a bobby pin.

Wig Application

Ventilated wigs (in which each hair is knotted separately into a net cap) are the best kind but are enormously expensive. If the budget is tight, cheap stretch wigs will do, especially when the hairline need not show. They come in a wide variety of colors and styles and can be doctored with braids, buns, and falls (pieces used to lengthen the hair in the back). Bald and semibald skin wigs are available, so that it is rarely necessary to block out extensive amounts of hair with derma wax—a messy and time-consuming business to engage in on a nightly basis.

Hair and hair wool (crepe hair) intended to match your own should be slightly lighter than your natural color, as false hair tends to go dull onstage. Secure wigs and hairpieces to tight pincurls on the scalp and see that all tendrils of your own hair are completely encapsulated by the wig or by a stocking cap worn under the wig. Wigs are dived into front first, then pulled down over the head and down in back. Clean off accumulations of spirit gum frequently with acetone or spirit gum remover so that the net edging lies flat against the face.

a   b   c

Fig. 69. Mercedes Ruehl accomplishing three character changes *(a, b, c)* in the same play merely by changing costume and hairstyle in *Fun House: A Victorian Carnival,* Four Winds Theatre documentary performed at the Statue of Liberty. Photograph *left* by Diane Quaid, photographs *center* and *right* by William McGonigle.

Facial Hair: Eyebrows, Mustaches, Beards

Adding facial hair is simple if you remember two rules:

1. *Bottom layers go on first to avoid matting the upper layers with spirit gum.*
2. *Keep all the hairs running in the direction in which they grow naturally out of the skin.*

Application

1. Comb out a moderate length of hair wool in at least two colors for maximum naturalness. You will not need as much as you would think. Wet and stretch it first, weighting it at both ends, if it is too curly for your purposes, until it is dry and flat, or iron it dry with a steam iron.

2. Mix the different colors well into a single hank and separate this into a number of small parcels (larger for beards than for mustaches, and note that the hair in beards is often darker in the underlayers). Spread out the hair with your fingers and flatten each parcel; then with scissors, snip off slightly on the diagonal one end of each of the flattened parcels. Lay the parcels out where they will not be disturbed by drafts or a careless elbow.

3 (fig. 70, mustache; fig. 71, beard). Apply spirit gum to a small area at the outer edge of the upper lip or eyebrow (in the case of a beard, in the center of the underside of the chin, about one-half inch back of the tip), as shown in figures 70 and 71.

4 (fig. 70, mustache; fig. 71, beard). Take one parcel of hair and stick down ONE END ONLY, the end you have cut on the bias. The rest of the length of hair must remain free of spirit gum. Press the gummed end down with an orange stick or wooden sculptor's tool. You will usually wait to trim until all the hair has been applied.

5 (fig. 70, mustache; fig. 71, beard). For a mustache, space the next parcel about one-fourth of an inch farther toward the nose. Repeat until you reach the center, then start the process over on the other side of the mouth. For a beard, continue the first layer around to both sides, then begin a second layer one-fourth inch behind the first, going farther down

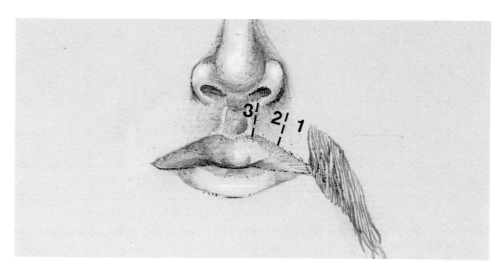

Fig. 70. Building mustaches.

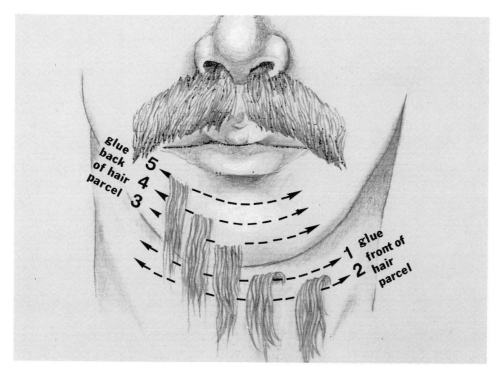

Fig. 71. Building beards.

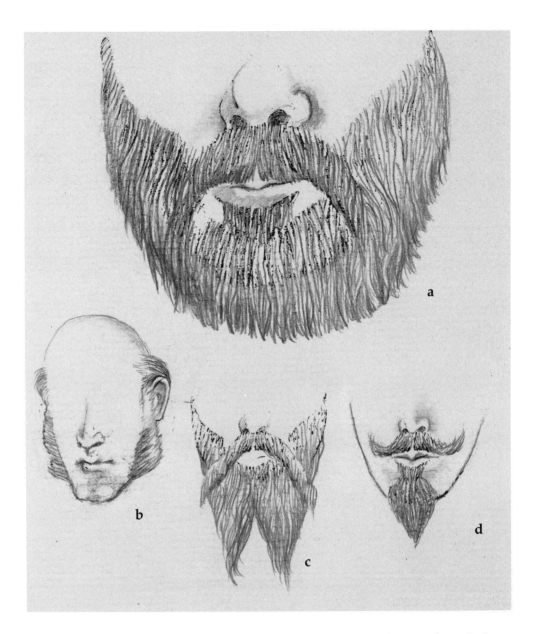

Fig. 72. *(a)* Full beard and mustache, mid-nineteenth century. Notice how darker hair in the underlayers gives depth and three-dimensionality to the whole. *(b)* Sideburns and beard, 1830. *(c)* Forked beard, sixteenth century. *(d)* Vandyke beard and mustache, seventeenth century.

the neck. If two layers here are sufficient, begin a layer just above the first, on the upper surface of the chin. Continue upward and to the side, each application overlaying the one below. Always follow the direction the hair would normally take on that part of the face.

If you are constructing both beard and mustache, leave them unconnected to facilitate normal jaw movement. Do the beard first, then add the mustache. Pull out stray hairs gently and trim to the desired shape. Hair may be lacquered to preserve order or deliberate disarray. (See figure 72 for examples of several styles of beards.)

Removal

To remove, brush spirit gum remover under the edge, pulling gently. Reusable facial hair can be built on a latex base painted directly on the skin (cover the natural eyebrows first with removable tape). Powder the inside of the construction as soon as it is peeled off, to prevent the latex from sticking to itself.

Reusable Constructions

You will have guessed by this time that applying facial hair is a laborious process, which is why many actors prefer to build facial hair on gauze or buy such constructions ready-made so that they can be peeled off and reused. The writer finds that the life of a reused eyebrow is short. They acquire a flat, dead roach look after a week or so. Mustaches also take a beating, but a well-made beard on gauze or net can be cleaned and should last with care.

Stubble and Five O'clock Shadow

Stubble or five o'clock shadow (figure 73) can be simulated with crepe hair scizzored into tiny bits and applied with adhesive. Alternatively, the illusion can be created by stippling with brown grease or pancake.

Fig. 73. Ken Tigar wearing stubble as a seaman in *So Long, My Tottie!* Four Winds Theatre documentary produced by the National Park Service.

Study Projects

1. Take three copies of a photo of yourself. They can be enlarged photocopies at least one-third life size. Out of colored paper, assemble a collage of three period hairstyles (men should include facial hair) and paste them around your face in the photos. See how each style affects the width or length of the face. (For ideas and guidance, on period styles, see appendixes B–G. This exercise can also be done on a computer.)

2. Do a before-and-after hairstyling for Eliza Doolittle or Jean Valjean or any other character whose appearance undergoes a radical change in the course of the play. Men: include facial hair. Women: build at least one set of eyebrows out of crepe hair for this project.

16

Outlying Areas: Keeping an Eye on Your Ears

There is no denying body makeup is, as the British say, a ruddy nuisance. It seems to have an affinity for every surface but the one for which it was intended. Applied to human skin, body makeup at once begins to fade, crack, streak, run, and puddle. Scorning flesh, it transfers itself quickly to the nearest object—handkerchiefs, collars, other actors' shirtfronts, your best coat. To these, it clings with the tenacity of indelible ink. It is no wonder that some actors will go to absurd lengths to avoid its use. However, when fully costumed, check all outlying areas for visible flesh. Novices betray themselves constantly by telltale patches of skin and hair. Unhappily, those to whom these patches are revealed are invariably the very people they wish most to impress—agents, producers, critics, mothers-in-law—all of whom are customarily ensconced in the first ten rows of the orchestra.

Spots to Watch

Get in the habit of checking the following areas as you apply your makeup, to avoid having to touch them up after hair and costume are in place.

- Creases around the eyes
- Depressions around nostrils
- Under the nose

- Hairline (all the way around)
- Under the chin, jawbone
- Throat and sides of neck
- Ears and behind ears
- Collarbone area and décolletage
- Hands, wrists
- Arms, legs, feet
- Any other part not covered by costume

Rules for making up these parts are the same rules of dark and light, hard edges and soft, as apply to facial structure.

Aging the Hands, Neck, and Chest

In age, the joints swell, tendons stand out, flesh sinks, and veins become more prominent (fig. 74). You need model only a few veins, not masses, and it is not sufficient to draw them on with a blue pencil as if you were making a road map. Like wrinkles, veins are three-dimensional and must have their shadows and highlights like other body features (see chapter 9).

Diminishing Exposed Areas

Costume can be used to cut down on the amount of skin exposed and therefore subject to body makeup. Mufflers, collars, leggings, bandages, scarves, gloves, and hats, like hairstyles, should be chosen with extreme care, as their primary objective is to abet the characterization, not to save the actor a few minutes' makeup time.

Study Project

Find a picture of a starving or extremely emaciated or elderly person. Make up your hands, neck, and chest to look like that person's. Don't just copy the picture. Feel for where the muscles, tendons, and veins are on your body and use the principles of highlight and shadow to emphasize them.

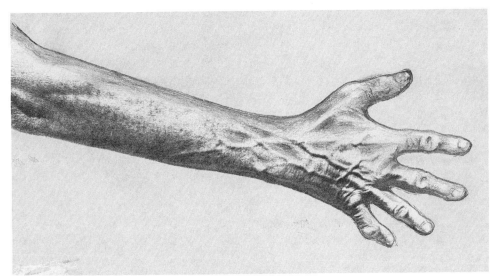

a

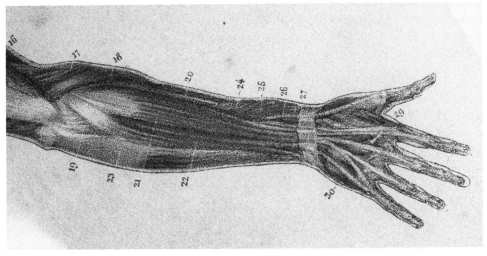

b

Fig. 74. Aging hands and arms: *(a)* Tense your hand to make the tendons stand out. Darken between them and also shadow sides of each finger. Outline the major veins in blue and shadow them on one side. Highlight veins, muscles, bones, and tendons at their highest points. Necks, arms, and other sections of the body: feel for the muscles and the bones underlying them. Sink in the hollows and add highlights exactly as you would for facial features. Use pictures or anatomical diagrams as guides *(b)*. Courtesy Richard Fitch, Americana.

17

Ethnic Particularization

As was said in part I, the concept of racial differences no longer holds much substance. At most, one can say that certain facial features are more prevalent in some parts of the world than in others. It may be useful to note that broad noses are characteristic not only of black people but also of Orientals, Hispanics, East Indians, and North Africans. Furthermore, even among those peoples, noses of every other shape are commonly found, so that no generalizations are possible to make about what any given individual will look like. Nevertheless, if the play's meaning depends upon faithful representation of a character's ethnic or national background, the actor's features ordinarily are expected to reflect that fact.

Unfortunately, universal agreement has not been reached on this question. Indeed, since the beginning of the 1990s Broadway and off Broadway have been inflamed repeatedly by controversy over the casting of ethnic roles with actors from a different ethnic group. Black actors have played Petruchio and Richard III without materially altering their features. Asians have played English lords. A Caucasian was barred by Actors' Equity from appearing in the role of a Eurasian.

There are those who doubt the actor's ability to cross ethnic lines convincingly. Others see the probing of an alien experience as the very essence of the actors' craft. Without arguing the respective merits of either side, this book is intended to assist actors of whatever color or national origin to conform their features to the image of their choice.

Fig. 75. Same actress as in figure 62, made up for a production of *The Good Woman of Setzuan*. Epicanthic flap over eye is done entirely with paint.

Common Variations

Appendix A illustrates the most common variations of feature within the species. It is intended only as a rough guide and should be supplemented by firsthand observation and pictorial research.

Conforming Your Features to an Ethnic Model

There is no difference in the techniques needed to slim a nose, widen a mouth, make an Anglo look Hispanic or an Italian look Chinese. Once the basic distinctions illustrated in appendix A have been comprehended, you are ready to create the necessary optical illusions. Go as far as you can with paint and hair alone, before moving on to derma wax or prostheses. Western eyes often have a modified epicanthic fold above the eye that can be accentuated for Asian characters (fig. 75). If your sockets are particularly deep, you can create the fold with a flap of gauze stuck on with adhesive or build one up with latex. Be careful not to get spirit gum in the eyes. Stick the flap down at both ends, leaving your own eyelid free to work normally under it. Make sure you can see easily. Skin color and skillful hairstyling or a wig are major factors in audience recognition of traditional or exotic cultures. If the character is darkskinned, the features will carry better if the base is of a medium value. In this way, the shadow color will not be too dark to be seen easily, and base, highlight, and shadow color can be better coordinated. (See discussion in chapter 5.)

Study Project

Make up as the character of a different ethnic background whose life and environment you researched for the study project at the end of chapter 5. If it is an Asian with an epicanthic fold above the eye, try to reproduce the fold in paint. If this doesn't work, make a gauze or latex flap. (Use pictures to guide you and refer to appendix A.)

18

Period Makeup

Viewing old Hollywood epics like *Antony and Cleopatra* and *Ben Hur,* is a lesson in paradox. How can such enormous sums of money have been spent for historical research with so little effect on the makeup? In chapter 4 the reader is reminded of how interdependent the parts of the body are. If a waist is corsetted down to fourteen inches, the cheek pales from lack of oxygen. When young men habitually fight on horseback carrying forty pounds of armor, they are unlikely to go about with chests caved in over an incipient pot belly, and it is probable that their robust physical condition will be be reflected in their faces.

Period makeup, then, transmits the habits of a society as formed by its basic philosophy and aesthetic tastes. Medieval women were expected to be fruitful—constantly—and appropriately submissive, accepting their role as the Virgin Mary accepted hers. Hence the swaybacked, jutting stomach stance, lowered eyes, and discreetly covered hair of the lady (i) in appendix C. In the Victorian era, emphasis on the comforts of home and on decorum helped to produce the staid, upright look we associate with that time.

Period clothing influences the face in many ways. Hair that is tightly drawn back affects the slant of the cheeks and eyes. A high collar changes the line of jaw and chin. A really authentic makeup signals that an in-depth study of the part has been made. When a classical play is done in modern dress, of course, the makeup will generally follow suit. If, however, historical accuracy has been studiously observed in the sets and costumes, respect for the integrity of the production calls for equal accuracy in makeup design.

A good way to get a feeling for what the face will do in period is to assemble from odd bits and pieces the elements of a costume typical of the time. Include jewelry, collars, lorgnettes, monocles, anything that works around the face. Paste on a paper mustache, move your hands "in period" after studying paintings of the time. Repeat into the mirror snatches of your most typical speeches from the play. As you slip into the character, face and body will assume the proper aspect, which, once observed, can be incorporated into the makeup design (fig. 76).

Fig. 76. Student creating an eighteenth-century character using bits and pieces of costume. Stella Adler Conservatory of Acting.

Heads from the main periods of Western history and some major eras in other parts of the world are illustrated in appendixes B–G.

Study Projects

1. Choose a character from a period play or imagine a character from a particular historical era. Study pictures of the time to see how the head was customarily held, whether facial hair was popular, etc. Design and execute a makeup that looks natural for that time. (There are periods in which cosmetics were heavily used and others in which the face was not made up at all.)

2. Add hair, pieces of costume, personal props, jewelry, etc., to complete the period makeup above.

19

The Realm of Fantasy

Mild Eccentricity

Eccentric literally means "outside of the center." It is used to describe people we find slightly odd but not certifiable. The eccentric is surprising or mildly startling. A woman wearing a hat at a luncheon, once fashionable, would be considered eccentric today. Boris Karloff's massive jaw and Eddie Cantor's pop eyes were facial eccentricities that became the actors' trademarks.

Crossing the Line into Caricature

When eccentricity is enlarged and distorted beyond what is possible in nature, particularly to make a political or social comment, it crosses the line into caricature. Lampoons of famous figures have been common to every age from ancient times to the present. (For examples, see figure 8, chapter 3, and figure 19, chapter 6.)

Hallucinating beyond the Species

Totally improbable combinations of features that remind us only distantly of the human face belong to fantasy (fig. 77). The three-faced girl in Ionesco's *Jack, or the Submission* is an absurdity in the real world. So are Francis Bacon's tortured images and *Peer Gynt's* trolls and the devils in the paintings of Bruegel and Bosch. So might be the makeups for Ariel and Caliban. Patti Labelle's coiffures in which hair is made to do the miracu-

Fig. 77. Student creating a makeup derived
from a bird image (a). Notice how she uses her
hands (b) and body (c) to assist her in finding
the character image.

The Realm of Fantasy   133

lous are examples of taking art and nature a step beyond into satire, caricature, and fantasy (figs. 78, 79, 80, and 81). Inspiration for such fanciful creations can come from sources as diverse as Naum Gabo's wire sculptures or a computer graphic (see chapter 6; for fabrication, see below, "Masks and Mask Makeups").

Fig. 78. A computer graphic can be the inspiration for a theatrical hairstyle (see figure 79).

Fig. 79. Katherine Ciesinski as Diana in *Calisto*. Photograph by Murrae Haynes, courtesy the Santa Fe Opera.

Fig. 80. Costume design sketch by Robert Perdziola for the Furies in *Calisto*.
Photograph by Hans Fahrmeyer, courtesy the Santa Fe Opera.

Fig. 81. Yarn wig worn by Olivia Cole in *The Hegge-Wakefield Nativity.*

Masks and Mask Makeups

Most masks follow the same technique of stylizing the human face by manipulating the features in imaginative ways or incorporating animal or plant motifs. Masks tend to be highly decorative and bold. Often the materials of which the mask is made are allowed to show their origins, and little attempt is made to reproduce the color or texture of living flesh. If the purpose were merely to reproduce the human face exactly, there would be no rationale for wearing most masks. Frequently, the colors or patterns used have symbolic meaning, as for example the Chinese use of red to indicate loyalty or sacredness, blue for craftiness, and orange to denote old age.

Nowhere than in masked drama is it more apparent how closely connected costumes and props are to the facial image. As Narsha C. Bol, a curator at the Museum of International Folk Art, says, "Mask and costume make a unit." She points out that some masks cannot even be constructed without the aid of costume. For example, the back masks of Mexico use a headress of cloth and feathers to camouflage the wearer's back and make it seem from behind as if he is facing front. Jaguar masks also illustrate this principle, it being impossible to tell where the mask

Fig. 82. Jaguar mask and suit made for a Mexican street festival. Painted wood and cloth. Oliver Velázquez Serrano, Suchiapa, Chiapas, Mexico, 1987. Courtesy Museum of International Folk Art.

ends and the costume begins (fig. 82). Teeth are contiguous to a long tongue that, in turn, drapes over a spotted neck that merges into the body of the beast. In this case, mask and suit are truly a one-piece garment.

Methods and Materials

Everything is grist for the mill of fantasy—rope, feathers, plastic, wire, steel wool, wicker, paper, any material, in fact, that gives the desired effect. Traditional base materials have included leather, wood, corn husk braiding coiled and sewn together, cloth, and yucca leaves (figs. 83 and 84). American Indian masks have bone, metal and tortoiseshell eyes and hair made of straw, horsehair, fur, and feathers. Other portions make use of basketry, wood slats, and eagle down. Even parts of human and animal skulls have been employed by mask makers. The writer once adorned a vampire mask with toy hand grenades and a head of the Devil with plastic grapes (they worked well for the early performances but deflated slowly during the run). For the mask of a pre-Columbian sorceress returned from the dead, she used sprayed and shredded plastic bubble packing, so that the face of the seer appeared to be dissolving in the light that shimmered off the fluttering pellets. To portray Yeats's evil Bricriu

Fig. 83. Kermit Love of "Sesame Street" helps a youngster to fabricate a mask. Ossining School District project.

Fig. 84. Completed mask
and cloak made from dried
weeds for *An American
Indian Thanksgiving Cere-
monial,* documentary
developed by the Four
Winds Theatre in coopera-
tion with members of the
Westchester Ballet for an
interage workshop, di-
rected by the author.

The Realm of Fantasy   139

(The Only Jealousy of Emer), she retrieved some foam rubber that had been in a fire that had produced masses of craterlike eruptions the color of mashed beetles. A half mask made from this substance suggested nicely the corruption of the character and went well with its scarlet spider's legs made out of a child's hoop. It is essential that all mask materials be lightweight. If stuffing or built-up sections are needed, styrofoam or some equally weightless substance will serve better than wood or metal. Papier-mâché is a traditional theatrical mask material and also one of the cheapest (fig. 85).

Fig. 85. Papier-mâché mask. Jesus Maria, Nayarit, Mexico, 1972. Courtesy Museum of International Folk Art.

Half Masks and Helmet Masks

Half masks have the advantage of leaving the actor's lips and jaw free, which much facilitates audience understanding of the lines (fig. 86). Full masks are confining but do not require the performer to make up parts of his face nightly to match the mask. Helmet masks cover the actor's head completely and are a necessity when the headdress is espe-

Fig. 86. Inga Nielsen and Scott Reeve in the American premiere of *The English Cat* by Hans Werner Henze. Courtesy the Santa Fe Opera.

cially heavy. This type of mask can be built on a football helmet, a ski mask or a cap that ties under the chin. Secure the underpinning first to ensure the mask an absolutely firm base. Hair can be sewn directly to this base. Some masks have movable jaws, eyes or ears, but these can be more difficult to engineer (fig. 87).

Ready-made Masks

A great timesaver is the use of ready-made Halloween masks as armatures. These are usually made of thin, hard plastic or of rubber and can totally be disguised by imaginative design that uses the features of the store mask merely as a support for further construction (an example is the mask of Satan, figure 24).

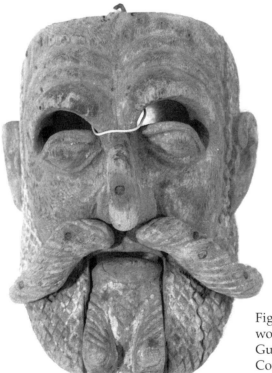

Fig. 87. Mask with movable jaw, wood with paint loss. Cruz Blanca, Guerrero, Mexico, pre-1950. Courtesy Museum of International Folk Art.

Boldness and Simplification

A clear, vivid depiction of a single character element is usually more effective than detailed realism or psychological complexity. That which cannot occur in nature can occur in a mask; it is from this that masks derive their special power and their fascination for children and adults. Nothing is too grotesque or farfetched as long as a mask communicates to its audience, as shown in figures 88 and 89. (For other examples of fantastic makeups and masks, see chapter 6.)

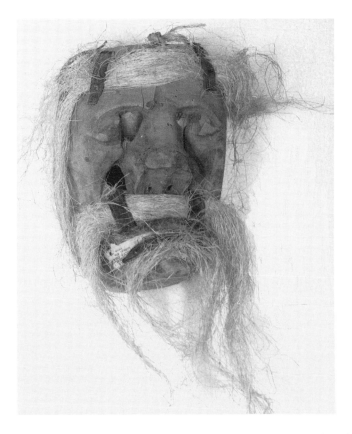

Fig. 88. Old man with sisal beard, unpainted wood with ixtle fiber. Michoacán, Mexico, ca. 1940. (Notice the fragment of a newspaper bound in with the mustache.) Courtesy Museum of International Folk Art.

Fig. 89. Dyak monkey mask from the collection of John Barker. Photograph by William McGonigle, courtesy Tom Riggs Gallery.

Study Projects

1. Execute the makeup for Ariel or Caliban that you designed for study project 1 at the end of chapter 6.

2. Construct the mask or mask makeup for a fantasy character from a children's book, a play, or science fiction that you designed for study project 2 at the end of chapter 6. Simplify as much as necessary to be able to complete the mask but stay faithful to the original concept. Perhaps other ideas for materials will occur to you. Be ingenious, but remember that the mask must be nearly weightless and must allow you to act without hampering either speech or movement.

3. Do a mask for one of the seven deadly sins. Draw on dreams, nightmares, plants, animals, fish, insects, or other sources that occur to you.

20

Costume and Prop Elements That Support the Image

It is easy to see how putting on bright green nailpolish can be at once an extension of the facial makeup, a piece of business, and a revelation of character. In this writer's opinion, not nearly enough thought is given to the ability of costume and prop elements to do these things—at least not by actors. Too often, it is the director who suggests an object or a piece of clothing that will enhance the characterization or serve the play.

Think for a moment of the objects that routinely work on or around your head: spectacles, earrings, a pencil stuck through a bun, your hat. There was a time when it was not possible to visualize Carmen without a red rose between her teeth.

A cigarette or cigarholder changes the shape of the face and the angle of the jaw everytime it is carried to the lips. Its size, shape, and color are therefore relevant considerations when designing the visual image. Negotiating a high collar or keeping a monocle in place requires ongoing muscular effort (figs. 90 and 91). Below is a partial listing of costume items and props that have an intimate connection with the facial image.

Fig. 90. Alan Gerstle in *Fun House: A Victorian Carnival*, coproduced by Columbia University and the Manhattan Theatre Club.

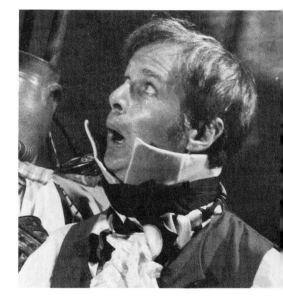

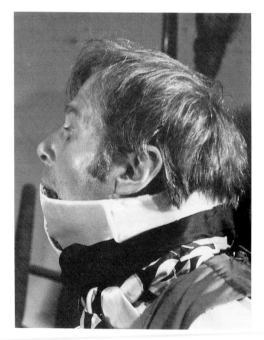

Fig. 9l. John Milligan makes good use of an absurdly high collar in *If Liberty Be There*, documentary on the Federalist controversy, written and directed by the author. (Costumes by Barbara Tholfsen.) Fanueil Hall, Boston. Photograph by Joseph Freeman.

Costume Elements and Personal Props
That Interact with the Facial Makeup

Costume Elements

Collars, ruffs
Cuffs, loose sleeves
Hoods, hats, snoods
Nets, veils
Hair ornaments, barettes
Combs
Flowers, feathers, plumes
Facial patches
Pendants, necklaces, lockets
Earrings, rings
Mufflers, scarves
Shawls, capes

Props

Cigars, cigarettes
Pipes, holders
Snuffboxes, pillboxes
Perfume bottles
Pencils, pens
Spectacles, sunglasses
Objects suspended:
    Opera glasses
    Lorgnettes
    Magnifying glasses
    Binoculars, cameras
    Pocket watches
    Pince-nez
Ear trumpets
Fans, handkerchiefs
A wad of bubblegum
A pet monkey

Study Project

For a role you are currently studying, make a personal prop that the character might wear or carry about him or her or use repeatedly (fig. 92). If you begin with something store-bought, alter it so that it becomes your creation. (If you intend to use it in actual performance, be sure and consult with the director before appearing with it onstage.)

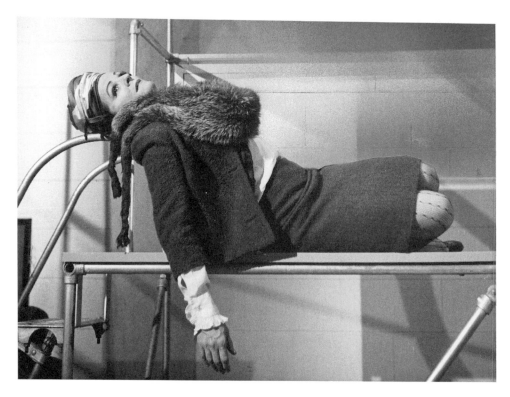

Fig. 92. Elizabeth Parrish demonstrates what can be done with two paws and a hank of fox hair. Buffalo Festival of the Arts.

21

Effects of Colored Light on Makeup

Technical discussions of this complex subject may be found in books on stage lighting and scene design. One bad experience will suffice to imprint on an actor's mind the general maxim that to avoid looking ghastly one must remember:

Cardinal Rule for Lighting and Makeup:
- *Similars attract.*
- *Reddish makeups need warm light.*
- *Green and blue makeups need cool light.*

Otherwise one risks standing onstage literally with "mud" all over one's face as the cosmetics so carefully applied go various shades of gray, purple, or brown. This applies to fabric also, as a young actress discovered in a recent adaptation of a nineteenth-century novel, when her gorgeous teal blue ballgown turned an unmentionable hue under candlelight. Before finalizing your makeup, talk with the lighting designer and see if imperceptible amounts of the color light you need can be added to a scene.

Primary colors of light (red, green, blue) are different from those of pigment (red, yellow, blue), so you cannot count on obtaining from light the color you would expect to get by mixing the same color paints.

General Guidelines

1. A gel of a given color will intensify makeup of the same color.

2. A gel of a complementary color will tend to darken and muddy the makeup color.

3. Dark gels will affect makeup more than light ones. Most lighting designers will therefore use gels like Straw and Bastard Amber (a light pink-orange) for lights that are focused on the players (see figure 58, chapter 10).

Study Projects

1. Arrange for two pools of light, one cool (blues and greens) and one warm (deep pink, red, yellow, orange, amber), to be turned on at opposite sides of the stage. (Alternatively, find some cast-off gels and do this in the dressing room or at home.) Hold swatchs of fabric of different colors under each kind of light. Note the color changes in the fabric.

2. Make a chart of the color changes you noted, keeping in mind, however, that some fabrics react rather unpredictably. Costumes and makeup should be tested under the lighting they will have in performance.

22

Sequencing and Revising the Makeup

Developing a Makeup Routine

The Working Diagram

Working diagrams are derived from an initial sketch that has been finalized (see figure 5, chapter 3). Below is a student's sketch for a character in Shaw's *Major Barbara*, converted into a working diagram (fig. 93) to be used as a guide while making up. The diagram need not be a great work of art, just a clear, uncluttered schema locating the highlights and shadows, identifying what colors are to be used, and noting facial hair if any. The information it contains should be in a form that you can grasp instantly under pressure, such as when you have five minutes to effect a major makeup change.

Testing the Makeup

During previews, it is wise to test the makeup under lights to make sure that the colors are not changed by the lighting designer's choice of gels, and that the features read as flesh and not painted wood. You can check this to some extent by taking a hand mirror onstage during the tech rehearsal, but it should be surveyed from audience distance by someone knowledgeable and friendly.

Checklist of Makeup, Costume, and Prop Changes

You need only recall what it felt like when you had to go on as an understudy on two hours' notice in order to realize how essential a check-

MAKEUP WORKSHEET

PRODUCTION: *"Major Barbara"*

CHARACTER: *Rummy Mitchens*

DATE: _____

PERFORMER: _____

TELEPHONE: _____

DERMA WAX or PROSTHESES *Derma Wax nose tip*	
BASE *Ruddy*	
SHADOWS *Red - brown* *Blue under eye*	
HIGHLIGHTS *White + base*	
ROUGE; STIPPLING *cheeks, nose tip* *Stipple for rough skin texture*	
HAIR: *dirty blonde,* **Head** *wispy, small bun, grey-* **Eyebrows** *streak* *build on gauze* **Mustache** *—* **Beard** *—*	
BODY MAKEUP: **Hands** *Redden on backs and age.* **Other**	

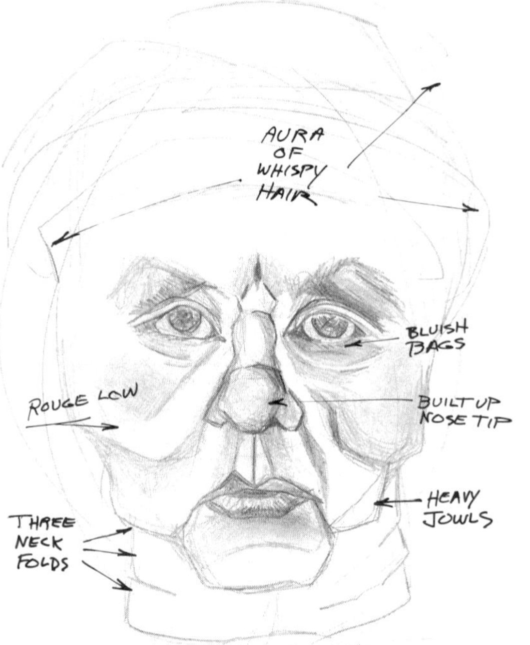

AURA OF WHISPY HAIR

BLUISH BAGS

ROUGE LOW

BUILT UP NOSE TIP

HEAVY JOWLS

THREE NECK FOLDS

NOTES:

Makeup *Broaden face to maximum; three neck folds.*

Costume *Use shawl and plaid scarf to camouflage neck, if necessary.*

Props *Fingerless gloves will cover most of hand.*
Dish towel tucked into belt

Other *Wedding ring.*

Fig. 93. Sketch by Charlotte Thorpe for the character of Rummy Mitchens in *Major Barbara,* converted into a diagram for the makeup worksheet.

list is. Performers have far too much on their minds to be able to think of details in the midst of the hurricane. Suffice it to say that a checklist of makeup, costume, and prop changes is a lifesaver, and that it must be comprehensive and legible in poor light. Also, a thumbnail sketch or photo taped to your mirror is worth a thousand words you do not have time to read, or cannot see without your glasses. Make several copies of the checklist and post it at all your entrances, as well as in the dressing room. Be sure to update it if there are changes.

Quick Changes and Mass Makeups

Speaking of changes recalls the time the writer was given a munificent one minute and twenty seconds to change out of a sweater, blouse, and skirt into a negligee and also turn the face of the character into one a few hours from death. All of this had to be accomplished in the wings, by flashlight.

Mass makeups have similar potential for nightmare: thirty makeups for the chorus of a production of *Lysistrata* leap immediately to mind. The solution to both situations is a good checklist and efficient design and sequencing.

If there is time, take front and profile photographs of the actors. The task of designing a makeup for each will be facilitated by laying tracing paper over the actor's picture and building your design from what each face offers naturally. Make sure the actor understands how to execute the makeup. If all of the makeups share a common style, you can demonstrate on one member of the cast while the others watch. Make it as easy for the actor as you can. Sew hair into the hats. Attach veils, crowns, and tiaras to wigs and headresses so that everything can go on in one piece.

Decide which things MUST be done and the order in which it would be best to do them. Then add a section of things to be done if there is time. In this way, the derma wax nose that changes character A into character B will appear onstage even if the false eyelashes don't make it. Don't even think of removing a base and starting from scratch. Just stipple with pancake and go on from there. If you cannot finish both highlight and shadow, brighten existing highlights or dab on new ones to give the basic effect. Makeup in pancake can be underlaid with another in grease, which will come to light when the film of pancake is washed off.

Simplicity is the watchword. If you do not have two hours to spend before the mirror, then you shouldn't have two hours' work to do when you fly offstage to change makeups or to assist others to do so. Select a few bold strokes that will have a major effect on the character and dispense with fussy details. If you have help, you can do more, but beware the day your dresser has the flu or falls down a flight of steps while en route to assist you. Lay out what you will need, with everything facing in the right direction in the order you will put it on. Like a fireman, you have to be down the pole and onto the runningboard in nothing flat.

Revising a Makeup during the Run

At the Broadway opening of Jack Gelber's play *The Cuban Thing*, mounted police were needed to hold the crowd at bay outside the theatre. Threats had been received from both sides of the Castro-Cuba controversy, and soon after the writer's first entrance, a voice rang out from the balcony: "I have a bomb!" Rip Torn quieted the hubub, the bomber was ejected, and the performance continued to the end, but we arrived at the theatre the next day to find a notice announcing that we had closed. For her character, a ninety-year-old Cuban matriarch, the writer, then a young woman, had designed after gargantuan struggle a makeup she considered her best to date. The only trouble was that she had conceived it after the opening, expecting to try it out on the second night. (She still has a silver cigarholder as a memento of the role but not a single photograph of that makeup, lost forever.)

The story illustrates what every actor is resigned to: the impossibility of "getting it all together" by opening night. Just as the role is never complete by an arbitrary date, so too the visual image matures with playing. As you improve the makeup, and after discussing major alterations with the director, transfer the changes to your working diagram and checklist.

Study Projects

1. Select one of the sketches you have made for makeups and convert it into a working diagram. Show colors to be used, where the highlights and shadows will go. Note hairstyle changes or false hair added.

2. Go through a playscript and note ALL personal props, articles of clothing, hair and clothing changes, jewelry, etc., worn or carried by one character. Make a list of these, scene by scene. Note on this checklist any quick changes or other problems you can foresee in performance. Use little thumbnail sketches to show what cannot briefly be described.

23

The Process Summarized

This book has explored a perspective on makeup that actors take for granted but cannot always carry into execution: the correlation of makeup and character. It has urged the necessity for the performer to take more responsibility for what the character looks like and to acquire the skills in application that will permit him or her to translate the visual image into reality.

Clues to that visual image abound in the play text, and the image is assembled from an initial impression of the text, followed by direct observation of people and objects or through the study of pictures. However, the performer does not work in a vacuum but develops the character image in cooperation with the director and designers. Gradually (in rare cases, quickly) the visual image takes shape, at which point the actor is well advised to get it down on paper in the form of a rough sketch so that the transient impressions garnered from the first and subsequent readings of the play and from the actor's research are not lost.

Working from real objects and from pictures, the actor sharp-focuses the image, distilling from animals, plants, and other sources of inspiration essences and specific details that carry out the visual concept. In the course of doing this, the actor emphasizes certain of his own features and deemphasizes others, making use of the principles of optical illusion to combat the flattening and bleaching effects of light and distance and to alter appearances.

Understanding that no part of the body is isolated from any other part, he visualizes the entire person and makes sure that the makeup reflects his idea of the character from head to toe. To ensure that this will be the case, he selects elements of costume and personal props that enhance the image. He or she makes sure the chosen hairstyle suggests not only period but the character's personality and social status as well.

Nationality and ethnic distinctiveness are difficult to generalize about but remain useful concepts if handled with sensitivity and restraint and when justified by the text. Theoretically, it is possible for any actor to create a convincing image of a character, no matter what his ethnic background or national origin. Whether, and to what extent, he or she does so with makeup is a matter for discussion with the director, whose overall production concept will govern here as in most cases.

Beyond everyday reality, the world of fantasy challenges the performer's ability to create dreamlike images that add another dimension to our perception of what exists or could exist. Here, especially, objects, plants, and animals, together with a wealth of materials both natural and manmade, constitute an endless source of inspiration to the imaginative actor.

Finally, the expansion of the actor's craft requires a corresponding expansion of his knowledge about makeup as it applies to other media. Even though a makeup artist is frequently on hand to aid him, the special requirements of film and television should be familiar to every performer.

Makeup for auditions, subtly applied, can be of material aid in suggesting a performer's suitability for a role. At the least, it presents the auditioner at his or her best to potential employers. Even the lecturer, while unconcerned with characterization, can nevertheless use makeup with discretion to project the features. Finally, the rules of stage makeup apply equally to makeup for street wear, with adjustments for the closeness of the "audience." Features can be enhanced, bone structure emphasized, and color heightened to convey an image of health, allure, or fantasy, as the spirit moves us.

Discussion of concept and style (part I) is complemented by "The Manual" (part II), which outlines ways and means to give form and substance to the actor's mental picture of the role.

Ultimately, it is not books, pigments, brushes, or crepe hair that achieve the character. Only the artist's vision can do that. Only the performer's drive to find that one face in a thousand can bring the visual image to birth and keep it alive and growing for the run of the play.

Appendixes
Index

Appendix A   Ethnic Distinctions

Frequent Features	*Also Found*
. . . . . . Straight black hair, sparse facial hair	Chinese
. . . . . . Epicanthic flap	Mongolian, Tibetan, Southeast Asian
. . . . . . Wide cheekbones	Slavic peoples
. . . . . . Aquiline nose	Arab, Aztec, South American Indian
. . . . . . Broad upper jaw	Black, Hispanic

Native American

. . . . . . Hair dark (straight or tightly curled)	
. . . . . . Pronounced brow ridge	
. . . . . . Dark eyes	
. . . . . . Wide nostrils, low nose bridge	Oriental
. . . . . . Broad upper jaw	Native American, Hispanic, South American Indian
. . . . . . Full lips	Australian Bushman, Arab

Black

. . . . . . Straight black hair, sparse facial hair	Native American
. . . . . . Epicanthic flap	(See Native American) Polynesian, Tibetan
. . . . . . Round, flat face	Eskimo
. . . . . . Button nose, low bridge	Black, Slavic peoples
. . . . . . Short "rosebud" mouth	

Oriental

.... Dark hair usual (but varies)

.... Dark brows

Hispanic, Italian,
others

.... Dark, heavy-lidded
deep-set eyes

East Indian, Persian,
Turkish, Ethiopian

Mediterranean

.... Hair color varies

.... Long, narrow, or
oval face

German, Scandinavian,
English

.... High bridge,
long, straight nose

Classic Greek, Roman

.... Thin, broad mouth

.... Prominent chin

Northern European

Appendix B
Period Styles: Middle and Near East, B.C.

Ancient Egypt, Assyria, and the Agean

Ancient statues and wall paintings emphasize the Egyptians' large, almond-shaped eyes, broad noses, high cheekbones, and full, well-defined lips (**a** and **b**).

For the most part, the people were straight, slim, and spare. They revealed their trim figures with form-fitting linen sheaths and loincloths, sometimes of fabric so finely woven as to be transparent (**c** and **d**).

Like their Cretan neighbors, women in the earlier Old Kingdom (ca. 2780–2280 B.C.) exposed their breasts. The short loincloth worn by men was later overlaid by an ankle-length skirt, and both men's and women's garments were heavily pleated. During the New Kingdom (ca. 1580–950 B.C.), the Asiatic seamed tunic (kalasiris) was adopted by both sexes.

Heads, ordinarily shaved smooth, were covered in public with black wigs by the wealthy and their attendants (**b**).

Egyptian ladies used a light foundation and were heavily perfumed. They reddened lips and cheeks, wore green eyeshadow, and outlined their eyes with a black substance called kohl.

Egyptians and Assyrians like this archer (**e**) were beardless, but Egyptian kings wore artificial ceremonial

beards, and both the hair and beards of Assyrian rulers were long and elaborately curled (**f**).

Cretan and Minoan figures display more sinuous, rounded lines than the Egyptians. Both men and women bared the upper torso, corsetting their slender waists with rolled leather belts.

Curls and spirals, major elements of Cretan art, were repeated in their undulating tresses, which the women embellished with ropes of jewels (**g**). They were reputed to be a light-hearted people much concerned with fashion.

h

i

j

k

Greece and Rome

Greek statuary of the Archaic period shows the same rigidity of pose that marks the Egyptians. Strict verticality later yielded to the supple, relaxed, yet disciplined, carriage appropriate to an athletic society whose motto was A Sound Mind in a Healthy Body.

Classic facial proportions (**h** and **i**) display deep-set eyes framed by curved brows descending to a straight or slightly aquiline nose. The space above the chiseled lips is rather small, the chin firm and prominent.

Softly draped chitons, increasingly rich and colorful, swathed their well-muscled figures (**j** and **k**).

Women's hairstyles ran from simple ponytails to elaborate chignons and top knots crisscrossed by bands and held at the back by nets of gold or silver (**l**). Men wore their hair long and carefully curled or in short locks that followed the shape of the head (**m**). Beards were pointed or square (**o**), but many men went clean-shaven.

Blond hair was achieved by the mostly

l

m

n

dark-haired Greeks through bleaching by both sexes. Cosmetics were heavily used by women, oils and perfumes by both men and women.

Early Roman dress was the same for both sexes: a large oval or rectangle folded and draped around the body. In time, women adopted a rather exaggerated version of Greek dress and hairstyles, heaping the hair in front into great tiaras of curls (**p**). Decorative combs, oversized hairpins, and bands of pearls preceded the heavy, jeweled diadems of the Byzantine period.

Tunics became popular, and as the wealth of the empire grew, clothing and accessories were increasingly ornate. At the height of Justinian's power in the sixth century, the loose linen and cotton tunics of the previous age were transformed into silken columns gorgeously embroidered, trimmed with wide ornamental bands, and set with many precious stones. The tunic was overlaid with enormous cloaks bordered in gold and held at the shoulder with a massive jeweled brooch (**n** and **q**).

o

p

q

a

b

Girls sewed, played the lute, and spun. The unhealthful times and possibly a lack of exercise, coupled with the doom-oriented outlook of early Christianity, made for pale, almost bluish, or yellow skin color and a fragile, attenuated look. Long noses, small chins, tiny rosebud mouths, and slender fingers were much admired among the nobility.

Before 1000, life remained hard even for the nobility. There were few comforts to mitigate the constant threat of plague and the disasters of war. Although strong-willed women like Eleanor of Aquitaine exerted considerable influence, the prevailing image of the female was a virginal and submissive creature with permanently downcast eyes and bulging

Appendix C
Period Styles:
Medieval to 1500

Middle Ages

The disappearance of classical culture brought enormous changes in fashion. Conquering barbarian tribes imposed an existence devoid of luxuries. Women's loosely fitting dresses and men's trousers and tunics were of coarse cloth sparsely adorned. With time, the dress (kirtle) became more formfitting and the trim-waisted doublet and hose became the fashion for men (**h**).

Men's hair was longer than in Justin-ian's time, and a mustache without a beard was common (**e**), although youths were often smooth-shaven; full beards, some-times forked, were also worn (**c** and **f**).

Young women wore their hair loose (**b**) or in thick single or double braids hanging down or coiled at the sides like giant ear-muffs (**d**). Early on, matrons covered the head with a loose drape. Whimples pass-ing under the chin concealed the neck (**g**).

Later, shaved eyebrows and foreheads (**b**) were set off by bulbous or sharply pointed headdresses (hennin) hung with gossamer-thin veils (**i**). Men's hair was also shaved above the ears (**a**).

c

d

e

f

h

i

abdomen, her carriage the typical posture of advanced pregnancy (**i**).

Men, of course, fenced, rode horse-back, and hunted in forty pounds of armor. Those who survived the recurring epidemics must have been a hardy breed with great endurance.

Early Renaissance to 1500

The Age of Chivalry and Courtly Love promoted fashions of extraordinary lavishness. Color, pattern, and ornament ran riot despite numerous sumptuary laws intended to restrain them (**j** and **k**).

Beards were of all shapes. They were usually short and carefully trimmed, although older men allowed them to fall almost to the waist. Young men wore their hair short, as in classical Greece (**n**), or in long, flowing tresses (**k**).

A more secular society showed its emancipation in garments daringly cut to expose the female bosom (**q**) and profusely puffed, slashed, scalloped, and trimmed.

Women's hair emerged from the confining hennin to be piled high and crisscrossed with ornamental bands (**l**) or dressed and curled in softly flowing locks and ringlets (**j**). Beards at this period were mostly worn by older men. The trend toward unrestrained enjoyment of wealth and privilege continued into the High Renaissance.

j

k

l

m

n

o

q

After gunpowder made armor obsolete, and as trade with the East brought great wealth to Europe, the clothing of the nobility grew more and more sumptuous, and their bearing prouder and more elegant. Fur was used extensively for trim and linings. The clergy (**o**, **p**, and **m**) continued to exert its influence, and increase its wealth.

Revived interest in the Greeks, the growth of exploration, and the rise of experimental science brought a relaxation of earlier attitudes toward women and gave them greater opportunity for education.

p

Appendix D
Period Styles: High Renaissance through the 1500s

The rise of the Italian city-states and merchant princes wrought startling changes in the facial image. Political ruthlessness and ecclesiastical worldly ambition are reflected in the piercing eyes and lean hard-driving look of the Medici and Sforza portraits of the time (**g** and **a**).

a

b

c

d

e

f

g

h

i

j

k

A counterbalancing emphasis on grace, piety, and sensitivity can be seen in the graceful hairstyles of Italian women (**b**), the delicate features of statues by Donatello, and the ascetic faces of the Church martyrs (**e**). Ruffs (**h**), stiff doublets, balloon breeches, and the codpiece enter the scene (**i**). Cloth of gold, cut velvet, and other rich fabrics of all kinds continued to be used, but the lines harden and confine both face and figure (**h** and **o**). Older men continued to wear long beards (**m**), but the young and middle-aged went smooth-shaven (**n**).

n

o

l

m

As usual, the clothing of laborers and peasants changed less and not as quickly. They wore more practical garments allowing freer movement (**j**, **k**, and **l**).

Weakened by decadence and the inroads of humanism, the Church struggled throughout this period to keep and increase its power, but the Reformation divided its adherents and led to the rise of the Puritan sect, whose dress was plain to an extreme (see appendix E, **m**).

a

b

c

d

Appendix E
Period Styles: The 1600s
(Baroque to Rococo)

Early 1600s

Cosmetics were used heavily, and once again front hair and eyebrows were shaved by women, a high forehead being considered a mark of

e

f

beauty (**b**). Hair was frizzed, but the exaggerated, built-out styles of the Spanish court (**f**) did not catch on in other European countries. Neatly trimmed mustaches and pointed beards were fashionable (**a**, **c**, and **e**).

Heavily boned bodices and hip-circling farthingales clamped women into an unbending carapace from which only their heavily jeweled fingers remained free (**d**). Men's breeches burgeoned into bells (**c**)

that later lengthened into modified sausages.

The posture of both sexes was uncompromisingly erect (**a**). Arrogant bearing and the unbridled display of wealth were the natural expression of fiercely nationalistic Europeans at the height of their intellectual, artistic, and economic power. As always, poor people's dress was layered for warmth and remained largely unchanged except for details (**g**).

g

Later 1600s

Spanish ruffs and the stiffened clothing that accompanied them gave place to more graceful, flowing drapery and hair (**i**). Décolleté for women (**j**) and broad mantles of exquisite lace on breast and shoulder, as well as at the cuff, characterize the period (**h**).

Beauty patches or false moles came in and remained popular through the next century. Primarily adornments, they also served to hide blemishes skin in an age when smallpox raged unchecked (**k**).

Men at first wore their natural hair long (**h** and **l**); women tied theirs in large chignons, leaving loose curls and tendrils dancing at the sides (**j**). After the "Sun King" made tall wigs fashionable (he was just over five feet), they became a standard item of dress and grew more varied and fanciful in shape and size with time (**n**).

Muffs were carried by both men and women, fans and masks mainly by women. Gloves continued to be an important accessory, and walking sticks appeared.

During the reign of Louis XIV the graceful garments of the men grew fussier, their unity fragmented by tier upon tier of ruffles, ribbons, and frills (**n**).

In contrast with the voluptuous, opulent swirls of art and fashion in the Baroque and Rococo eras, Puritan dress was sober in color, plainly cut, and without ornamentation (**m**).

169

Appendix F
Period Styles: The 1700s (Rococo) and Early 1800s

The 1700s

The excesses of the age of absolute monarchy led to political upheaval and ultimately to radical changes in fashion and the place of women in society. Rationalism and scientific advances in the Age of Enlightenment fostered intellectual achievement by both sexes: this is the century of the great salons and increased recognition of female achievement in literature and art.

Court dress remained elegant. Panniers held women's skirts out at the sides to widths that were satirized in cartoons of the period. Stiff bodices and tight waists pushed up the bust. Gracefully positioned arms and hands emerged from tight sleeves ending at the elbow in bursts of lace (**c**).

Men wore flared coats ending at the knee, left open to display the waistcoat and set off by lace at throat and wrist (**d**). Both sexes wore high heels. Snuffboxes, lorgnettes, and for women the parasol and ubiquitous fan, were common accessories.

Women and some men painted outrageously with white lead and other dangerous or malodorous preparations.

Powdered wigs the size of over-grown pumpkins (**c**, **h**, and **g**) were worn by both sexes after the initially simple hairstyles of Watteau's

time (**b**). Men were mostly clean-shaven (**a**), but older men wore long sideburns, and older women covered the head with bonnets (**e**).

It was an age of great wit, and precious manners reminicent of the Rules of Courtly Love. Coquetry, raised to a high art, made adultery seem an innocent pastime. Inevitably, sentimental fantasies about shepherdesses and their swains were shattered by bloody revolt and the destruction of a glittering, brittle society.

Later in the century, skirts were shorter and their fullness gathered to the back, revealing delicate ankles and moderately high-heeled shoes (**g**).

Wigs gave way at the century's end to the windswept look of the Napoleonic era, which imitated Greek and Roman hair and dress.

Early 1800s

Men's collars rose to new heights (**o**), and short tight jackets displayed the long line of the leg, encased in close-fitting light trousers and boots (**m**). Swords were exchanged for the whip or walking stick (**i**).

The Terror swept out corsets and high heels, ushering in a daringly relaxed way of dressing, notable for an increase in the amount of female flesh that could be publicly displayed. Feminine legs and bosoms could be distinctly seen through partial coverings of transparent material (**l** and **p**). Ease of civil marriage and divorce at this time provided a further indication of the new freedom enjoyed by women.

Country women hiked up their skirts, rolled up their sleeves, and otherwise adjusted a homespun version of the fashion to the practical demands of milking, cooking, and caring for children and animals (**j**). Large shirts and smocks were worn by peasant men, along with vests, loose trousers, and caps of various shapes (**k**).

One of the most graceful and simplest of fashions, the high-waisted Directoire and Empire dresses in light cotton or muslin were usually complemented by a long shawl (**l** and **p**). This was also the era of great capes and overcoats (**n**).

Women's hair and sleeves became ever more bouffant and elaborate. The wider the sleeves, the more sloping the shoulders appeared, giving a boneless look to the upper torso and exposing more nape (**q**).

After 1840, women's hair was dressed more simply, tending to be parted in the middle and slicked close to the head from crown to temple.

The small, pointed beards and mustaches of the 1830s (**r**) were enlarged during the course of the century into mutton chops. Full beards and sideburns remained popular almost to the end of the century (see appendix G, **a**).

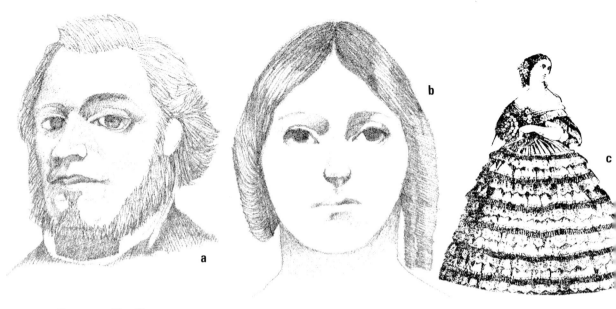

Appendix G
Period Styles: Mid-1800s through the 1900s

Mid-1800s to 1900

Facial hair was popular for men, and beards of all shapes and sizes could be seen (**a**). Lush side-burns and a wind-swept look, with the hair brushed forward over cheeks and forehead or curling away to the sides, characterized the Civil War period (**e** and **g**).

By the 1860s, skirts had ballooned into great half spheres supported by crinolines (**c**). Then they narrowed again to the bustle gowns of the 1880s (**d**) and the even narrower and more staid high-buttoned black jacket and skirt combinations of the early 1900s (**f**).

Hair, coyly center-parted and smoothed by the Victorians (**b**),

was piled high by women of the 1880s (**d**) and gathered into a pompadour in the 1890s (**f**) before being bobbed by the courageous in the early decades of the next century (**q**).

Given fourteen-inch waists and the hourglass figure, it is little wonder that the nineteenth century was also the age of smelling salts and fainting spells.

Men's dress dwindled by the end of the century into a basic suit of unre-markable shape and somber color, precursor of the corporate "gray flannel" worn by the modern business executive (**h** and **i**).

j

k

l

The 1900s

Not notable for its sartorial flamboyance, the early twentieth century quickly reduced the great cloaks and capes of the nineteenth century to the overcoat, the trench coat, and, by midcentury, the leather jacket and unisex jeans.

Eager feminists had already bobbed their hair (**q**).Makeup, frowned upon in the Victorian era except by ladies of the Moulin Rouge, was back in favor by the time of the flapper (**k**, **o**, and **q**).

Women's fashion reflected their broadened role and political emancipation. Clothing allowed greater movement as women swam, rode, fenced, played golf and tennis, skated, or rowed (**m**). Bloomers, introduced earlier with little success, became popular, and skirts shot up

m

o

p

above the knee with the advent of the Roaring Twenties.

Men's clothes underwent fewer changes, but the sweater, soft-collared sport shirt, slacks, and patterned jacket brought variety and freedom from the tyranny of black and gray formal attire (**r**).

Mustaches and beards continued in fashion (**j**) until the smooth, peeled look of the 1920s temporarily banished them (**p**). With World War II came the men's crew cuts of the 1940s, followed by the bow wave of the 1950s. Long hair and beards returned in the 1960s, along with more flamboyance and individuality in dress, and have remained an option ever since.

In the 1940s women's hair and skirts were briefly longer (**n**), then shorter, and finally largely a matter of individual choice.

Today, male and female hairstyles and clothing are frequently interchangeable (**l**) and the eclecticism of the closing decade of the century is typified by one fashion reporter's opinion that "the consensus is: no consensus" and by designer Josie Natori's dictum: "Today there are no categories or boundaries in fashion."

n

q   r

173

Index

Page references to illustrations are printed in boldface type

reasons for wearing, xvii, 3–4; rebellion against, xviii; research for a, 14–16; starting a picture file for, 16; stylized, 47–60, 132–44

Makeup design: animals and objects as sources, 20–22, 26–29, **27, 28,** 50, **52, 58, 133;** asymmetry in, 31, **31;** clues to, in the script, 11–13; designing a facial landscape, 19; director's and designer's input, 14; drawing from your sources, 19; emphasizing a feature, 29–31; factors to consider, 16–17; impressions, 19–24; outside sources for, 14, 16; period and style influences on, 13–14; physical givens, 11, 13, 34; plastic constructions, 32 (*see also* Prostheses); sharp-focusing the image, 29

Makeup execution: aging from childhood on, 104, **105, 107;** applying the base, 79; blending, 95–96; bones and muscles in, 73, **74, 75,** 124–25, **125;** changing the features, 97–100, **98, 99;** checklist of makeup, costume, and prop changes, 151; child characters, **74, 104–7, 105, 107;** corrective, 109–12, **111;** equipment and materials, 69–72, **70,** 77–78; face preparation, 78; facial planes, 73–76, **74, 75;** mass makeups, 153–54; mixing main colors, 77–78; period makeup, 129–30, **130,** (*see also* Period styles); practice exercises, 80–81, 82–83, 84–85, 86–87, 88–89, 90–92; principles of application, 77–79; quick changes, 34, 153–54; revising a makeup, 154; routine for, 151; sequencing the makeup, 153; stippling, 95–96; testing the makeup, 151

Makeup materials. *See* Equipment and materials

Makeup routine. *See* Sequencing the makeup

Makeups, mass. *See* Mass makeups and quick changes

Makeup sketches. *See* Drawings and sketches

Masks and mask makeups: animal and plant motifs in, 50, **51, 58, 133, 137, 138, 139, 141, 144;** boldness and simplification, 143; costume and mask, relation of, **52, 55,** 136–37, **137;** designing masks and mask makeups, 53, **54, 57, 59,** 136–44, **138, 139;** freedoms and constraints, 53; half masks and helmet masks, **56, 141;** masked characters, 53; methods and materials, 137–40, **140, 142, 143;** ready-made masks, 142; suprahuman characters and archetypes, 54, 60, **58, 59;** symbolic meaning, 54, 136

Mass makeups and quick changes, 153–54

Mastergate, 49

Montand, Yves, 4

Morse, Robert, 4

Mother Courage, 13

Moulage, 102

Mummenschantz, 60

Muscles of face and body (*see also* Body makeup): face and neck, **75;** arm and hand, **125**

Musical theatre, makeup for, **52, 55, 56,** 62–63, **64, 134, 135, 141**

Mustaches and beards, 113–16, **114, 115,** 118–22, **119, 120, 122**

Nationality (*see also* Ethnic makeup): basic distinctions, **162, 163;** Maria Benitez on, 41–45, **42;** conforming your features to an ethnic model, 127–28, **127;** ethnic particularization, 126–28; legitimate concept or baseless fiction, 40; national images, 40–46

Nonnaturalistic makeup (*see also* Masks and mask makeups): beyond naturalism, 47; fantastic makeups, 50, **52;** heightened and slanted characters, 48, **49;** making a social or political comment, **28,** 49, **49;** satire, comedy, farce,

fantasy, and, 48–49; suprahuman characters and archetypes, **52,** 54, **58, 59;** theatre of the absurd, 47; *Nose, The,* 56

Objects, taking from animals and, 26–29

O'Casey, Sean, 47

Odets, Clifford, 47

Old age. *See* Age

Opera, makeup for, **52, 56,** 62–63, **64, 134, 135, 141**

Optical illusion, principle of in makeup, 76–77, 97

Othello, xvi, 13

Outlying areas. *See* Body makeup

Pancake, interchangeability with greasepaint, 93

Papier-mâché (*see also* Masks and mask makeups: methods and materials), 140

Parrish, Elizabeth, **148**

Peer Gynt, 4–5, 49

Pélléas et Mélisande, 34

Period styles, **164, 165, 166, 167, 168, 169, 170, 171, 172, 173, 174, 175;** customs of, and makeup, 129; effect of, on makeup, 13–14, 129–31, **130,** 145–47, **146;** elements of costuming, 129–31, **130;** hair (*see* Hair and hairstyles: period styles)

Photographs, makeup for, 61–62

Picture file, starting a, 16

Plough and the Stars, The, 11, **27**

Pouches. *See* Age: wrinkles, folds, and bags

Powdering (*see also* Makeup execution), 84, 86, 92

Props: checklist, 151–52; as extension of the makeup, 15, **15,** 36–39, **37, 38;** importance in developing the role, 35; personal props and costume list, 147; that change the face shape, 145, **146;** worksheet, **152**

Prostheses: decision to use, 32; preformed, latex, 101–2; put-

Jenny Egan began her career as actress, director, and teacher by winning the Clarence Derwent Award for her performance on Broadway in *The Crucible.* She created roles in the American premieres of plays by Albee, Arrabal, and Ionesco and has played featured parts in television and films. She was an assistant director with the New York Shakespeare Festival (under a Ford Foundation grant) and the Lincoln Center Repertory Company, and was makeup consultant to both. Trained by Stella Adler and Standford Meisner, she taught at the Columbia Graduate School of the Arts, City University of New York, New York University, where she earned her doctorate, and was visiting professor and master teacher of acting at Southern Methodist University. She has written and designed extensively for documentary theatre, including her own company, The Four Winds, with which she toured in this country and abroad, and has directed straight plays, opera, and musicals. Her film *In Freedom Born* was a finalist at the American Educational Film Festival. At one time Illinois fencing champion, she is married to a systems analyst.

Reed Campbell is an artist living in Santa Fe. He received a B.A. degree in painting and printing at Fort Wright College of the Holy Names in Spokane and an M.A. degree at the University of New Mexico. He has exhibited in Santa Fe and Washington and is an instructor in printmaking at the Santa Fe Graphics Workshop.